My Lord and My God

My Lord and My God

Engaging Catholics in Social Ministry

JEFFRY ODELL KORGEN

Foreword by Jack Jezreel

PAULIST PRESS
New York/Mahwah, NJ

Cover design by Trudi Gershenov
Book design by Lynn Else

Library of Congress Cataloging-in-Publication Data

Korgen, Jeffry Odell.
    My Lord and my God : engaging Catholics in social ministry / Jeffry Odell Korgen.
        p. cm.
    Includes bibliographical references and index.
    IBN 0-8091-4370-4 (alk. paper)
    1. Church work—Catholic Church. 2. Lay ministry—Catholic Church. I. Title.
    BX2347.K67 2007
    261.8088'282—dc22

                                                    2006016475

Published by Paulist Press
997 Macarthur Boulevard
Mahwah, New Jersey 07430

www.paulistpress.com

Printed and bound in the
United States of America

Contents

Acknowledgments vii

Foreword by Jack Jezreel ix

Introduction: *"I'm Talkin' about JESUS!"* 1

PART I
Invitation: *"Follow me!"*
    1. The Social Concerns Committee That Works 17

PART II
Conversion: *"My Lord and My God!"*
    2. The JustFaith Phenomenon 35
    3. A Journey to Justice 55
    4. Global Solidarity and the Middle Pew 72
    5. Young Prophets of Justice 88

PART III
Empowerment: *"Feed My Sheep"*
    6. Broad-Based Community Organizing 107
    7. Worker Justice 126

Conclusion: *Are You Talkin' about JESUS?* 143

Notes 146

To my parents,
Benjamin and Judith Korgen

Acknowledgments

We are lucky to have lived when giants still roamed the earth. This book would not have been possible without them. They are people like Msgr. Jack Egan and Margaret Roach, Msgr. Philip J. Murnion, Sr. Helen Prejean, John Carr, and Ronald Krietemeyer. Their professional godchildren are some of the most inspiring people I have ever worked with, the Roundtable Association of Diocesan Social Action Directors. This book is based on the work of these Catholic diocesan peace-and-justice directors. Roundtable members provided valuable background and many leads for interviews. They continue to challenge me with their wisdom and sustain me with their abundant fellowship.

This book also could not have been written without the challenge and support of the Outreachers, a peer supervision group of Catholic social ministry staff from a number of national organizations. I wish to thank Joan Rosenhauer, "Big Dan" Misleh, Donna Grimes, Tom Chabolla, Kristi Schulenberg, Tom Ulrich, Rachel Lustig, and Mary Wright for sparking the Outreachers' conversation that led to this book. Several of the Outreachers also provided valuable leads that brought me to the exceptional disciples profiled in these pages.

Three organizers with the Industrial Areas Foundation provided valuable leads and vouched for me as I interviewed leaders of their organizations: Mike Gecan, Marielys Divanne, and Sr. Kathy Maire. To those who agreed to be interviewed for this book, I thank you for speaking so candidly about your lives. Your words continue to inspire me after so many readings. I hope that I have done justice to your stories here.

Thanks to the editors and readers who gave such honest and helpful feedback, beginning with my editor-of-first-resort,

Kathleen Odell Korgen, and Fr. Gene Lauer at the National Pastoral Life Center. Paul McMahon of Paulist Press provided invaluable advice, editing, and support. Mary Wright and Matt Gladue offered helpful advice on the final manuscript. Kudos to Jack Jezreel for his work on the foreword.

A special thanks to Metro-North Railroad for providing a cell-phone free zone in which to write. And a final thank you to Julie and Jessica Korgen: you girls offer me so much joy and hope that the kingdom of God will be realized, here and there, in your lifetime.

Foreword

JACK JEZREEL

One paraphrase of Jesus' teaching that Dorothy Day often referred to in her column "On Pilgrimage" in *The Catholic Worker* goes, "We love God only as much as we love the person we love the least." The phrase articulates, with exhilarating and excruciating clarity, the Christian conviction that our love of God must be manifested in a kind of broad love of our sisters and brothers that takes into its embrace the concerns of all and the good of all.

Dorothy, perhaps *the* American Catholic prophet of the twentieth century, understood herself to be speaking a basic truth to a church that seemed, simultaneously, inspired by and disinterested in the message of Jesus' teaching and life about the way to know communion with God. It was a church that in some places, especially communities of men and women religious, nurtured holiness and compassion for the poor and vulnerable, but it was also a church that, in its local parish form, was all too often all too silent and disinterested in human suffering and need. Dorothy's passion was not just to ensure that people got fed or housed or loved; Dorothy was concerned for the integrity of the tradition and, more immediately, was anxious that God's people were distracted from the very message that would bring light, life, and communion with God.

Dorothy was not interested in social ministry as one available choice in a kind of cafeteria line of ministry options offered at the local parish. Social ministry—motivated, in part, by the recognition of God in the tug toward the poor/wounded/vulnerable and in the work and linkage of compassion—was the *only* available option to those who would call themselves Christian. The dream of Vatican II, I think, speaks not of a church with a social mission, but a social mission that has a church, a people. Faith, Eucharist, and prayer—understood and experienced fully—all necessarily draw us into and are intimately connected with the work of justice, caretaking, charity, and peacemaking. As the US Catholic bishops testify in the rousing document *Communities of Salt and Light*, "We cannot be called truly 'Catholic' unless we hear and heed the Church's call to serve those in need and work for justice and peace."

What was affirmed in the theology of Vatican II and stated with growing force and definition by popes and bishops for the last forty years is that the work of compassion, charity, justice, and peacemaking needs be an integrated part of parish life. Why? Because it is what Jesus preached. It is what Jesus did. It is what Jesus calls us to do. It is the way we experience communion with God.

As theology has moved gradually from the vision of prophets, popes, and bishops to implementation in local parishes over the last few decades, the process has been difficult; it has been a bit like putting new wine into old wineskins. Remarkable as it is, what was instigated in Vatican II and what continues in the emerging theology of social mission is not merely the description and prescription of an additional ingredient, namely, social ministry, for an otherwise adequate blueprint for parish life. What has happened in these last four decades is the redefining of the very reason for the parish's existence. This is not a recipe born of a hope that an occasional parish will offer a social ministry, among its many other ministries, to those few who might be interested. Rather, the parish itself has been given a new identity, a redefined purpose, a restored mission. New wineskins for new wine. And the mission is, not surprisingly, to be about the embrace of the reign of God, to be about the work of God's love and justice. This justice proclaims that all God's people are precious, and we are called to arrange our lives and our world to speak a great amen to that fact. Everything else in the parish would somehow have to integrate that mission or be deemed of marginal importance.

As parishes and dioceses have worked to make this vision and mission come to fruition, some things have worked, some have not. And when they work, the impact has been exciting and worth noting and celebrating. This book is about exciting things that are well worth noting and celebrating and imitating.

Jeffry Odell Korgen has assembled in lively and engaging fashion stories of social ministry successes, best practices, invaluable hints, and precious wisdom about ways to make the life-giving work of social ministry exactly that. You will find in these pages an extraordinary compilation of the most potent, life-changing, effective strategies for engaging the church in its own mission. From community organizing to formation to reverse missions, it is all here. If you are looking to make social ministry work where you are, this is the book.

And the particular insight that fills every page is that recognition that social ministry is really a matter of *metanoia*. New life, new sight, being born again—all gospel emphases—speak to a new way of being in the world. God is ever calling us to new possibilities, next steps, and deeper union. One of social ministry's tasks—perhaps its most critical task—is to speak and invite to this new possibility. Social ministry is about the recognition of God and God's call in this world of suffering. Social ministry, at its best, is really about evangelization—calling people to a new vision, a new way of being and living, a new birth into a new life. It is necessarily about invitation, conversion, and empowerment—the titles of the three main sections of this book. Social ministry is gospel ministry.

What makes all of this trustworthy is the parade of voices the author has assembled for the reader that attests that the gospel invitation is about the vision of justice as life giving. Not only can it heal and bring life to the world where there are wounds, but it brings new life to those who hear and heed the call.

Finally, and significantly, Jeffry Korgen has set in front of us not just options that we can choose or not; he has set before us the blueprint for a vital and vibrant American Catholic Church. Those parishes that do not heed what is herein described, I fear, may find themselves distracted and committed to lesser causes; happily, those that make this book a touchstone of pastoral strategy will make their way to deeper meaning, critical work, local and global solidarity, and a relevant spirituality. Sounds like gospel to me.

Introduction

"I'm Talkin' about JESUS!"

My favorite subway evangelist preaches beneath Grand Central Terminal in Manhattan. Each morning, she starts my day with the same sermon, delivered in the familiar cadence of the great African American preachers.

> I'm not talkin' about the pope.
> I'm not talkin' about your pastor.
> I'm talkin' about JESUS!

How often, I think, as I cross through the turnstiles, do we who work for social justice get so caught up in the issues, so obsessed with the political process, so consumed with the internal troubles of the church, that we forget about Jesus?

> He's Prince of Peace,
> Lord of Lords.
> I'm talkin' about JESUS!

My mind wanders to a meeting of the Catholic Campaign for Human Development (CCHD) Committee at the United States Conference of Catholic Bishops. CCHD is the largest funder of community organizing in the United States and a leader in social justice education. As a CCHD staff member describes the campaign's "how to" suggestions for parish justice-education leaders, Bishop Bernard Schmitt of the Diocese of Wheeling-Charleston listens intently. Finally, he interrupts, "The problem is that you people jump to the 'how to' when my people aren't even at the 'want to.'"

Amen, Bishop Schmitt! As secretary to the Roundtable Association of Diocesan Social Action Directors, I have heard many of my colleagues from Catholic dioceses across the United States describe parish evening programs on Catholic social teaching attended by six people, social justice lobby days in which seven Catholics represented a diocese, and parish social concerns committees composed of one person. In many parishes social ministry efforts are moribund or worse. "Nobody cares." "Everyone is so apathetic here." "People are just too busy these days." These statements are what you hear from the stalwarts who stick it out, those one-person committees. To these social justice advocates, the "want to" problem is all too apparent.

My evangelist interrupts this depressing monologue:

I don't care if you're a Seventh Day Adventist.
I don't care if you're a Baptist.
I don't care if you're a Catholic.
I'm talkin' about JESUS!

"I'm talkin' about JESUS!" Could this subway evangelist be answering Bishop Schmitt's question? I enter an open car and take over the sermon as the subway doors shut:

I don't care about your knowledge of Catholic social
    teaching.
I don't care about your expertise on social justice issues.
I don't care about your pastoral plan.
I'm talkin' about JESUS!

How do we respond to Bishop Schmitt's problem of the "want to"? How do we draw new leaders into the church's social action ministry? Dr. Donald Emge, social action director for Missouri's Diocese of Springfield–Cape Girardeau suggests that for the church's social action ministries to be successful, they must engage the "middle pew." The middle pew contains neither "social justice nuts" nor "right-wing zealots." They are ordinary people with many responsibilities who seek a closer connection to God, but often find it difficult to make time for church commitments outside of Mass. Rich and poor Catholics sit in the middle pew, and all of the church's racial/ethnic groups find a place there.

A good place to start thinking about how to engage the middle pew is with what works. There is plenty of bad news out there, but here and there, in pockets of surprising energy, you find people who get it right. Parishioners leave meetings full of energy and the Holy Spirit. The "quiet one" learns how to chair a meeting of seven hundred people. Professionals change careers because of an experience of finding Christ in the poor. The number of people engaged in social ministry expands geometrically over a period of years. The common thread, I have found, is simply an experience of Jesus Christ.

> He's Prince of Peace,
> Lord of Lords.
> I'm talkin' about JESUS!

Without the direct, personal experience of Jesus Christ, parish social justice committees remain anemic—alive, but hardly building the kingdom of God. Jesus points the way forward, through his words and actions in the gospels. That is the message of this book: I'm talkin' about JESUS!

The chapters ahead present the organizing methodology of Jesus as a paradigm for engaging Catholics previously uninvolved in social ministry. We look at models that successfully draw parishioners from the middle pew into a passionate charism of working for social justice. We examine how these models function, and explain *why* they are effective. In each case an experience of Jesus draws new leaders into social action, through *invitation, conversion,* and *empowerment.*

Invitation: *"Follow Me!"*

For some Catholic social justice leaders, Jesus calls "Follow me!" (Matt 9:9) through the mouths of other Christians. These sisters and brothers in Christ invite them to greater challenges of discipleship based on knowledge of their gifts, needs, interests, and desires. Chapter 1 describes the dimension of *invitation* in the organizing methodology of Jesus, as revealed through his own development of the apostles. We explore the implications of Jesus' method of *invitation* and learn how to apply it successfully in Chapter 1.

Do you advertise social ministry opportunities in the parish bulletin, asking (pleading?), "Are there any volunteers?" Do you grow increasingly bitter about the poor response? If so, you need Chapter 1! We examine a relational approach to organizing social justice ministries, employing the one-to-one relational meeting to connect with new leaders. We meet Bertha, the amazing one-person social concerns committee, who carries the entire salvation of a parish on her shoulders. We contrast Bertha's approach with a healthier model developed in the US bishops' *Communities of Salt and Light*. Lessons drawn from the best practices of parish and broad-based organizing groups provide concrete applications of the salt-and-light model to parish life.

Conversion: *"My Lord and My God!"*

Among disciples called to social action ministry, some develop a passion for social justice that derives from a personal experience of Christ in the poor. These Catholics stand like Thomas, who, after missing Jesus' first appearance to the apostles, insists, "Unless I see the mark of the nails in his hands, put my finger in the mark of the nails and my hand in his side, I will not believe" (John 20:25). When Jesus again appears to the apostles a week later, he says to Thomas, "Put your finger here and see my hands, and bring your hand and put it into my side, and do not be unbelieving, but believe." Thomas replies in wonderment, "My Lord and my God!" (John 20:27–28).

Through a face-to-face encounter with poor and vulnerable people, these disciples glimpse the Christ of Matthew 25. You might recall the scene presented in Matthew 25:31–46. It is the Last Judgment, and Christ has come into his glory, with all the angels surrounding him. Christ the King judges people as a shepherd who separates the sheep from the goats. Jesus addresses the righteous sheep:

> "Come, you that are blessed by my Father, inherit the kingdom prepared for you from the foundation of the world; for I was hungry and you gave me food, I was thirsty and you gave me drink, I was a stranger and you welcomed me, I was naked and you gave me clothing, I was sick and you took care of me, I was in prison and you visited me." (Matt 25:34–36)

The righteous ask Christ when it was that they fed, clothed, and visited him. Jesus replies, "Truly, I tell you, just as you did it to one of the least of these who are members of my family, you did it to me" (v. 40). Then, he turns to the goats and says,

> "You that are accursed, depart from me into the eternal fire prepared for the devil and his angels; for I was hungry and you gave me no food, I was thirsty and you gave me nothing to drink, I was a stranger and you did not welcome me, naked and you did not give me clothing, sick and in prison and you did not visit me."
> (Matt 25:41–43)

The goats, echoing the sheep, ask when they ignored Jesus' needs. Again, Jesus replies, "Truly I tell you, just as you did not do it to one of the least of these, you did not do it to me." The gospel continues, "And these will go away into eternal punishment, but the righteous into eternal life" (Matt 25:44–46).

Some Catholics are drawn out of the middle pew and into a passionate commitment to social justice through a face-to-face encounter with this Christ of Matthew 25. In that utterly intimate experience of the Savior, these disciples cry out "My Lord and my God!" Their faith comes alive with passion for the wounded Christ, found in the hungry, the thirsty, the sick, the imprisoned, and all of their postmodern variants. It is quite literally an experience of salvation.

Chapters 2 through 5 explore social ministry efforts that promote such encounters with Jesus Christ. These programs bring

Catholics into dialogue with poor and vulnerable people within the context of the study of scripture and Catholic social teaching. Chapter 2 examines "JustFaith," a thirty-week formation process that counts over seven thousand graduates throughout the United States. CCHD's domestic-poverty education/formation program "Journey to Justice" is the focus of Chapter 3. Chapter 4 looks at three very different encounters with people living in poverty around the world, and Chapter 5 examines social justice conversion experiences within youth and campus ministry service-learning programs.

Each of these ministries brings participants face to face with the Christ of Matthew 25. In so doing, they develop new leaders from the middle pew in their a commitment to social justice. What they each have in common is a twin commitment to the study of Catholic social teaching and scripture *and* to encounters with Christ in the poor and vulnerable. Taken individually, these elements do not typically engender conversion. Studying Catholic social teaching and scripture alone can lead to right thinking but no action; justice stays in the head. By the same token, an encounter with the poor alone can simply reinforce stereotypes. Together, the study of Catholic social teaching and scripture *combined* with a direct experience of the poor has jolted many Catholics out of the middle pew, crying "My Lord and my God!" at the feet of the wounded yet glorified Christ.

Empowerment: *"Feed My Sheep"*

Most conversion efforts in social ministry are aimed at middle- and upper-income Catholics. By contrast, some low-income Catholics see *themselves* on the cross and resolve to live as resurrection people, leading broad-based community organizations and worker justice groups. These Catholics have already put their hand in Jesus' side, and Christ may well have appeared to them in the form of a neighbor or family member, Indeed, they may have even glimpsed Christ in the mirror, through their own suffering.

For low-income Catholics the church carries out the commitment of Peter, whom Jesus instructed, "Feed my sheep" (John

21:17). The flock includes poultry workers, residents of burned-out cities and border *colonias*, mothers of teenaged victims of violence, and desperate family farmers. Over a century ago the church began to articulate, through Catholic social teaching, that "feeding" involves much more than giving alms. Feeding the flock also demands helping people with little power to develop some. This work can be controversial, but as the late Cardinal Meyer of Chicago said to famed community organizer Saul Alinsky, "There is nothing more controversial than a man hanging on a cross."[1] Again, the Catholic Campaign for Human Development has played a substantial role in how the church in the United States feeds the flock, drawing thousands of low- and moderate-income Catholics out of the middle pew and into social action ministries. In addition, hundreds of pastors and parish ministers with a charism for empowerment have helped low- and moderate-income Catholics develop the power to change their communities and work places.

Chapters 6 and 7 demonstrate the application of Jesus' tool of *empowerment*. Chapter 6 examines the effects of broad-based community organizing and its role in developing new leaders for social action ministry. Chapter 7 focuses on the church's empowerment of low-wage workers through worker organizations and parish actions. Like Chapter 6, Chapter 7 lifts up lessons for engaging low-income Catholics in the church's social ministry.

The Carpenter's Toolbox

In many respects the three strategies described above are intimately related. *Invitation* is typically what brings Catholics to the *conversion* experience or down the road of *empowerment*. Once fully engaged in social ministry, those who once cried out, "My Lord and my God!" in a moment of *conversion* invite others into public discipleship. Likewise, those *empowered* by the church want to "Feed my sheep," and *invitation* is their most effective tool. They may also wittingly or unwittingly participate in the *conversion* of others.

Jesus was a carpenter. He knew that it takes different kinds of tools to build a complex structure. He left us a toolbox[2] of sorts, through his words and actions in scripture. You have probably done some simple carpentry on your own. After you saw a piece of wood, you must put your saw down and pick up a hammer to fasten the wood to another piece. In social ministry we do the same, here drawing tools of *invitation* from the carpenter's toolbox, there removing tools of *conversion*, now utilizing tools of *empowerment*. It is all part of the same project: building the kingdom of God where God's justice reigns.

A Stew of Motivations for a Public Life

It is impossible for me to write a book like this without reflecting on my life and why Catholic social ministry has become my own charism. In the pages that follow I will ask you to reflect candidly on your own motivations. I will invite you to meet with others and relentlessly ask them who they are and who they are becoming. Like Jesus, you must know people before you invite them into deeper levels of discipleship. That knowledge begins with the understanding that we are complex people with varied motivations. Part of owning that is recognizing the "stew" of motivations that underlies your commitment to justice.

One of the most important realizations for me as a social minister has been that a mix of interests drives my commitment to social ministry. Like it or not, we are all motivated by complicated desires. The most dangerous people are those who recognize only idealistic motivations in themselves, or those who see a single reason, typically either very admirable or quite "victim" oriented, underlying their commitment to social ministry. We humans are a stew of needs, interests, and desires. Some ingredients keep their shape and form yet affect the overall flavor. Others dissolve and invisibly integrate into the overall flavor.

The reasons for my own passion for social justice include laudable qualities: a concern for others, a desire to bring about the kingdom of God, and a wish to carry on the moral legacy of my parents. But they also include parts of myself that I do not feel especially proud of: a desire to be well known and well liked, a tendency toward grandiosity, a loathing of boredom, and a lifelong need to make people laugh. I have come to believe that the more selfish of these interests do not negate the idealistic, but only humanize them.

Like most people, I received a lot of my values and passions from my parents. My father grew up in a neighborhood in Duluth, Minnesota, designated for foreign-born (largely Serbian) steel workers. Grandpa was foreign born; he arrived from Norway when he was three years old. And Minnesota's housing discrimination against immigrants extended even to Norwegians. Dad gave me a concern for the "little guy" that was certainly forged in that tough Iron Range neighborhood. He also taught me that patriotism is perfectly compatible with a desire for peace and belief in military restraint. Dad served the Navy for a quarter century, four years as an enlisted man during the Korean War and twenty-one years as a physical oceanographer for the Naval Oceanographic Office, earning the nickname "God of Currents" for his understanding of the seas. Knowing intimately the costs of war, Dad saw the use of force as a last resort among the tools of foreign policy and transmitted that just-war ethic to me.

My mother grew up as the belle of a small town in Michigan, daughter of a respected family physician and a no-nonsense homemaker. Mom experienced great privilege in her upbringing but also believed in extending those privileges to all Americans. Mom could say "That's not fair!" because she was raised on the idea of meritocracy and believed in it. I used to think her naive, but now I realize that her unwavering belief in the American values of freedom and fair play gave her the power to speak up when governments, businesses, or civic organizations did not measure up to those ideals. I have since met other seemingly naive people in social ministry whose moral outrage gave them the courage to stand up to a bullying mayor or persuade a reluctant congresswoman to switch her vote on debt relief. When Mom reached the "glass ceiling" in corporate life, she joined various women's movements for economic and social equality. She was the first of many feminists to shape my public and private lives.

Beneath this strength of character my family was quite fragile. For reasons that I still do not completely understand, we have experienced more than our share of mental illness. In many ways it was the experience of living in a house full of vulnerable people that led me to develop a passion for the struggles of poor and vulnerable people. I would be lying if I left myself out of that category. I was very confused by the emotional challenges that the family faced during my grade-school years. In that confusion I telegraphed vulnerability to the predators of the schoolyard and became a victim of bullying. When I was twelve years old the first stirrings of adolescence helped me fight back and learn the power and solidarity of organized people.

As a child, did you ever find your school lunch soaked in tobacco juice? I did. In seventh grade a bullying incident changed my life. It was the late 1970s, and my family was part of an influx of new residents drawn to the Gulf Coast by the oil and space booms. Old South met New South, or collided, in Slidell, Louisiana, a small city near New Orleans.

Slidell's Clearwood Junior High School was strictly tracked. Student tracking was one way that segregation lived on after *Brown v. Board of Education*. Our school added a new twist, segregation by social class in addition to race. Our guidance counselor arranged the seventh grade into four groups:

White middle-class and upper-middle-class students	7–D
White working-class and poor students	7–C
African American middle- and working-class students	7–B
African Americans living in poverty	7–A

Two students who resisted placement in this structure by being Chinese American and Mexican American were placed in 7–C.

Tracking occurred in every class except physical education and industrial arts, which those of us in 7–D shared with 7–C. In shop class, while we in 7–D worked on our ashtrays, three boys in 7–C stole lunches out of selected 7–D students' desks and spit tobacco juice on the food.

Chewing tobacco was a fad that had spread quickly among the boys in sections C and D. It seemed as if the school administration quietly approved. When two boys vomited after swallowing their chaws, our health teacher taught us the proper way to chew, "See, y'all ain't doin' it right. Y'all gotta put it in 'tween your cheek and gum lak this, see?"

I didn't like the humiliation of these incidents, and I sure didn't enjoy the experience of hunger. But how could I fight back? These were tough guys, and I mostly fought with words. I worried obsessively for weeks, terrorized by the randomness of the roughly twice-weekly attacks. I spent more time thinking about how to respond than I did on my schoolwork. I eventually found an answer in social-studies class. We were studying NATO, with the zeal of a generation that had convinced itself that nuclear war was pretty darn likely. Interest in the relations between the Soviet Bloc and the Free World was high. I was intrigued by the notion that under the NATO treaty, an attack on one member would be considered an attack on all NATO members. It seemed to have rich application to my situation.

I was convinced that I couldn't fight back alone, but if an attack on one could be considered an attack on all, weren't there ten of us being victimized by three? And if we isolated them one by one, wasn't that ten against one? I liked those odds! If you have ever seen the cartoon of the big fish eating the little fish and then being eaten by a school of fish arranged to look like a still larger fish, you have a sense of my thinking.

The ten of us broke the code of the schoolyard and began talking about tobacco juice terrorism. We signed a treaty and created an organization. We surrounded each boy at recess and told him that the attacks had to stop, or *he* would have to deal with all of us together. Tobacco juice terrorism ended on that day!

Years later, when I attended the Industrial Areas Foundation (IAF) ten-day training, community organizer Gerald Taylor explained the two kinds of power in public life: organized money and organized people. It did not take long for me to catch on. I kept thinking of my first experience of the power of organized people and the intoxicating effect of vanquishing not one bully but three.

When I reflect on those earliest experiences of public life, I can identify the seeds of my passion for Catholic social action, but these memories strike me as utterly secular. Certainly some of my parents' spirituality and values got through, but I had no enthusiasm for God, Jesus, or church whatsoever. My only prayers were that my parents would oversleep and we would not have to attend church that week. In return, I promised God to watch two episodes of *Davey and Goliath*. As I grew older, the pressure to go to church subsided, and there was only modest encouragement to attend the church youth group. I went once, but I had difficulty understanding what raising money for a ski trip had to do with Jesus. I didn't even ski. We were in Louisiana, for God's sake!

And then I placed my hand in Jesus' side.

When I graduated from Slidell High School, I considered myself a Christian, but I doubted. I was a Christian one day and an agnostic the next. I was eighteen years old and ready to begin an adventure at Boston College, a school that I had chosen in spite of its Catholic tradition, because I thought, "It's cool that they require you to take philosophy." When I preregistered, I signed up for a double philosophy/theology course called PULSE that included a ten-hour per week social-service placement. I signed up for the Norfolk Prison Fellowship, the most exotic sounding opportunity. Each week a group of undergraduates drove to a medium-security prison for discussions and fellowship with the prisoners. They were the inmates; we were the "outmates." At first I was scared of the prisoners, and they were indifferent to me, much more interested in my female classmates. Most were murderers, in for life. I learned that by asking what their sentences were. I never asked what crime they had committed. When someone tells you that he is in prison for life, you know the crime. Only the brutality of it is left to the imagination.

In time the inmates became more human for me, as I did for them. I became less "B.C. Guy" and more Jeff, this kid from the South who was less affluent than most B.C. students and who shared the inmates' passion for reading every article in the *Boston Globe*. I started to see the scared, vulnerable side of these men. The inmates who volunteered for the Norfolk Prison Fellowship tended to have resigned themselves to life in prison, but they wanted some meaning and friendship in their lives apart from their prison experience. Some seemed to want to atone for their sins through good works within the walls. The fellowship was one way they maintained the energy to continue that project.

Late in the year, the men asked me to chair a meeting. This was a great honor, usually reserved for one of the older inmates. I turned the offer down twice before agreeing. I was scared, fearful that I would let the group down by suggesting an uninteresting or "weird" topic. I decided to take a risk by asking a question that had been burning in my heart for weeks, "How do you find meaning in prison life?"

In that discussion I saw an even deeper vulnerability in the men. In prison for life, this question was the undertone of every day. One inmate, Malik, who was serving two life sentences, spoke of his great loneliness, interrupted only by these weekly meetings. I looked at him and for a moment, just a flicker of a moment, I saw Christ.

In the car returning to Boston College, I was very quiet. A classmate noted that I was not talking constantly, as I usually did. I turned my face to the glass and quietly wept. "My Lord and my God! My Lord and my God!" On that day I became a Catholic.

A moment of conversion. Like Thomas, my belief in the risen Christ was always conditional, wavering on agnosticism. And now Jesus sat in front of me in the most unlikely of places, a chat group for murderers. Looking back, it would be simplistic for me to say that all I needed to find Jesus was to attend the Norfolk Prison Fellowship. I also needed the guidance of the church. Indeed, my classroom experience was essential. Our PULSE class, "Personal and Social Responsibility," required reading scripture, Greek philosophy, and contemporary religious books such as Rabbi Harold Kushner's *When Bad Things Happen to Good People*. I do not think I would have seen Christ in Malik's face without having studied Matthew 25 and all of the other readings earlier in the year. At the moment of conversion it seemed that each of the class readings had been preparing me, all along.

In truth, I had met Jesus many times before but never recognized him. I was like the disciples on the road to Emmaus (Luke 24:13–35). My moment with Malik was the breaking of the bread, the opening of my eyes. I honestly believe that without the readings, without the support of fellow students, and without the guidance of our professor, Father Phillip Jacobs, my conversion never would have occurred. I stood, like Thomas, before Christ and, no longer doubting, called out, "My Lord and my God!" This was no ski-trip fundraiser, I thought; *this* was religion!

But this book is not a memoir. *I'm talkin' about JESUS!* I share these stories with you as a reminder that all of us bring a complex stew of histories, needs, interests, and desires to discipleship. The experience of Jesus mediates each set of motivations in a different way.

- Why do *you* work for justice?
- Why do some issues animate you more than others?
- What are some of the motivations for your work in social ministry that others don't see, perhaps because you keep them hidden?
- When and where have you glimpsed Christ?

Jesus left us a winning methodology in the scriptures for engaging new leaders in social ministry. Adopting his tools begins with self-knowledge, asking oneself these challenging questions. Take a moment now and write out your responses to the questions on the following page. I used to skip over exercises like these in books, but I'm convinced that you will find this helpful as you proceed. The first chapter underscores the notion that if you want to organize like Jesus, you need to know people at this level before calling out "Follow me!"

PART I

Invitation:
"Follow Me!"

1

The Social Concerns Committee That Works

The first tool that we borrow from Christ's toolbox is *invitation*. When Jesus called "Follow me" (Matt 9:9) in the gospels, he employed a relational organizing methodology that still works today. Indeed, it is the only approach that consistently gets results. In the chapter that follows we look at the most common vehicle for organizing parish social ministry, the social concerns committee, with a view toward drawing new leaders from the middle pew into these committees. We explore how to use the 1-1 relational meeting to invite new leaders into social ministry and to develop them over time, much as Jesus did with his disciples. We begin with an introduction to someone you may already know: Bertha, the amazing one-person social concerns committee.

Don't Be a Bertha!

Rich Fowler, former Archdiocese of Washington social action director, was making the rounds, meeting with each pastor in the archdiocese. He sat across from a pastor of a mid-size parish and asked, "Do you have a social concerns committee here? The priest broke into a wide smile and replied, 'Oh, you mean Bertha! Bertha's great! She would be a big help to you! I don't know what I'd do without Bertha!'"

Bertha? She *was* the social concerns committee! Perhaps when the Last Judgment of Matthew 25 occurs, Bertha will join a select flock of sheep in heaven. Her lonely toil will ultimately be rewarded. And she will say to the goats, "I gave you many opportunities to feed Jesus, but you did not read the bulletin. I offered you a chance to give Jesus a drink, but you did not listen to the announcements. Depart from me, you accursed, into the eternal fire prepared for the devil and his angels!"

I'll admit it. I was a Bertha. I moved into the social justice center at Boston College after my conversion and joined an elite group of martyrs, each convinced that we were going to save the world through our agitating (and irritating) tactics. We agitated and irritated our fellow students and the B.C. administration, convincing ourselves of our moral superiority. We lived in a state of political correctness before the term was even invented. At the end of a year I was burned out, and Boston College closed the house. As smug as I felt, I knew that I was not the same person who had cried, "My Lord and my God!" I had become a bitter Bertha indeed, and the next year I began a long journey back to spiritual health.

Are you a Bertha? Do you carry the church's social mission on your shoulders? If so, you are not doing anything particularly holy; instead, you are robbing other Christians of opportunities for salvation. When you put notices in the bulletin, do you blame those who do not come forward or yourself for not having a more imaginative strategy to engage new leaders? I'm talkin' about JESUS! Did he gather disciples by putting notices in synagogue bulletins or fishermen's newsletters?

Berthas make two fundamental mistakes. First, they try to develop social justice ministries with methods that treat people as things, as subjects awaiting assignment, and ministries as slots to be filled. Second, they adopt a posture of moral superiority vis-à-vis other parishioners, always attributing their inability to engage parishioners to the moral failings of the congregation. Ironically, a ministry that is about helping others thus becomes a supreme act of self-absorption and quite ineffective.

Rule #1: Don't be a Bertha.

Communities of Salt and Light

In their 1993 document *Communities of Salt and Light*, the United States Catholic bishops present a compelling alternative to Bertha's approach to social ministry. The bishops introduce a seven-faceted social ministry model, maintaining that "we need to build local communities of faith where our social teaching is central, not fringe; where social ministry is integral, not optional; where it is the work of every believer, not just the mission of a few committed people and committees."[1] In a community of salt and light the work of social justice and peace is not limited to the "social justice nuts" or the Berthas, it is also the work of the middle pew.

A community of salt and light may indeed be led by a small group, but these leaders must also draw others into parish peace and justice ministries. The bishops write, "We are called to be the 'salt of the earth' and 'light of the worlds,' in the words of the scriptures. This task belongs to every believer and every parish. It cannot be assigned to a few or simply delegated to diocesan or national structures. The pursuit of justice and peace is an essential part of what makes a parish Catholic" (4).

The bishops present "a framework of integration" in the document, seven elements of the social mission, each requiring special attention. Together, these elements help the parish become a community of salt and light:

1. Anchoring Social Ministry: Prayer and Worship: Good liturgy helps the faithful "recognize Jesus in the breaking of the bread and those without bread" (5). Without good liturgy and prayer experiences, social ministry leads to burnout. The relationship between worship and action is an intimate one, best articulated in scripture by James, who cautioned, "Faith without works is also dead" (Jas 2:26).

2. Sharing the Message: Preaching and Education: Those who preach ought to take advantage of the many opportunities afforded by the lectionary to reflect on the social mission of the church. The bishops do not suggest that preachers become partisan, but instead exhort them to use lectionary readings to teach about biblical justice and the principles of Catholic social teaching. In addition, all of a parish's educational programs, from children's religious education to adult formation, should present Catholic social teaching alongside other major doctrines of the church.

3. *Supporting the "Salt of the Earth": Family, Work, Citizenship:* Catholics act on the church's social mission through parish ministries, but we must not ignore the everyday choices made by the faithful in the arenas of family, work, and citizenship. The church must support parishioners in living justly every day by (1) assisting families in raising children who live by gospel values, (2) helping workers and managers bring Christian values into the marketplace, and (3) encouraging leadership in civil society, including "community groups, unions, professional associations, and political organizations, at a time of rising cynicism and indifference" (7).

4. *Serving the Least of These: Outreach and Charity:* Reaching out to the poor and vulnerable through direct service is a gospel witness that Catholics do quite well. Indeed, after the federal government, Catholic Charities is the largest provider of human services in the United States. Soup kitchens, prison outreach, food pantries, and assistance with rent and heat are a few of the staples of parish social ministry.[2] To be sure, these ministries are essential to the social mission of the parish, but we must not limit ourselves to "outreach and charity." The bishops explain: "A parish serious about social ministry will offer opportunities to serve those in need and to advocate for justice and peace. These are not competing priorities, but two dimensions of the same fundamental mission to protect the life and dignity of the human person" (8). Here the bishops make it clear that social ministry is incomplete if we only respond to the direct needs of people who are suffering; we must also address the causes of their suffering through action in behalf of justice.

5. *Advocating for Justice: Legislative Action:* An essential part of promoting citizenship is encouraging participation in electoral politics. This encouragement may include nonpartisan voter education and registration, parish events convening candidates and parishioners for discussion about the issues of the day, and religious education about the importance of civic engagement. The parish must also help Catholics organize to be a voice for "vulnerable children—born and unborn—on behalf of those who suffer discrimination and injustice, on behalf of those without health care or housing, on behalf of our land and water, our communities and neighborhoods"

(9). The bishops make a clear distinction between being "political" (advocating on the issues) and being "partisan" (endorsing or otherwise favoring individual candidates). The former is an essential part of a community of salt and light; the latter is prohibited by church teaching.

6. *Creating Community: Organizing for Justice:* One of the substantial ways in which the church promotes the empowerment of low- and moderate-income Americans is by funding community organizing projects through the Catholic Campaign for Human Development (CCHD). Catholic parishes also provide key leadership in hundreds of faith-based community organizations across the country. Communities benefit from these organizations as neighborhoods rebuild and resources flow to community-designated priorities. Parishes benefit as new church leaders develop, the areas surrounding churches become safer, and parishes find new opportunities to act on gospel values and Catholic social teaching.

7. *Building Solidarity: Beyond Parish Boundaries:* "Who is my neighbor?" the scholar of the Law asked Jesus (Luke 10:25–37). In *Communities of Salt and Light* the US Catholic bishops remind us that answering that question demands overcoming "barriers of race, religion, ethnicity, gender, economic status, and nationality" (10). As members of a global church, Catholics are in a unique position to become bridge builders. A parish's participation in twinning programs or partnerships with other parishes around the world, its involvement with Catholic Relief Services' projects like Operation Rice Bowl, its advocacy for peace, its work on racial justice at home—each is a testament to solidarity.

The US bishops present *Communities of Salt and Light* modestly. It is *a* model, not *the* model, according to the statement. Yet, over a decade later, no alternative paradigms have emerged. Many resources that complement *Communities of Salt and Light* have come along, but no one is suggesting changes to the basic paradigm.

I think the bishops got it right the first time, particularly in their insistence that the whole of the parish must be involved in the social mission. It is easier to cast this role to a marginalized committee rather than to do the tough work of making "justice...constitutive to the preaching of the gospel."[3] Thanks to the US bishops we have a compelling model of social ministry, but for this paradigm to be successful we must return to the problem of engaging the middle pew.

Jesus Christ, Organizer

How do we build communities of salt and light? I'm talkin' about JESUS! I asked earlier in this chapter if Jesus put notices in the synagogue bulletin. Of course not! Instead, he called, "Follow me!" (Mark 2:14) to prospective disciples. In short, Jesus invited potential leaders, based on a relationship.

Too often, we ignore Jesus' example in our parishes. We develop what some colleagues have called an instrumental approach. We treat people as objects, not subjects—worker bees, not disciples of Christ. We ask for volunteers; we place notices in the bulletin. We identify slots to fill. E-mail and the World Wide Web have simply given us new ways to treat the faithful as things. Bertha can now add "I sent e-mail to every parishioner" to her revision of Matthew 25.

A relational approach offers a methodology closer to Jesus' own. It begins with a conversation. The organizer (you!) asks questions, learns people's stories, what "makes them tick." An organizer talks about mission but is not selling anything. With some understanding of potential leaders and their interests, the organizer invites them to attend a meeting or take some other specific action.

Jesus said "Follow me!" at the beginning of his public ministry, but as he came to know the disciples—their skills, their interests, and their shortcomings—he took the next step and invited them into deeper levels of leadership. Consider an event as simple as the naming of the twelve apostles (Luke 6:12–15), a very public act of invitation. Picture the scene: Jesus' public ministry is well under way. After a long day of preaching he leaves the disciples for a night in prayer at a nearby mountain.

> And when day came, he called his disciples and chose twelve of them, whom he also named apostles: Simon, whom he named Peter, and his brother Andrew, and James, and John, and Philip, and Bartholomew, and

Matthew, and Thomas, and James son of Alphaeus, and Simon, who was called the Zealot, and Judas son of James, and Judas Iscariot, who became a traitor.

We can only imagine what the selection of the apostles must have been like. We know from Luke that Jesus prayed about it. It must have been a difficult decision, requiring the assistance of the Holy Spirit, but it also required a deep understanding of the strengths, weaknesses, and interests of those twelve men.

Some scholars focus on the ordinariness of Jesus' selections—simple men going about their lives, fishermen, laborers, and *even* a tax collector. I would argue that Jesus did not choose the apostles for their ordinary qualities but for what he saw as extraordinary within them. What was it that Jesus saw in Simon when he renamed him Peter (*petra*, "rock")? This is the disciple who sinks like a rock after walking on water with Jesus. This is the disciple who denies Jesus three times. Yet Jesus found something in Peter on which he was willing to stake the fate of the church. And he was right!

When you develop your church's social ministry, when you build that community of salt and light, you have to be like Jesus. You have to look for people with leadership qualities. You are not after "joiners," folks who sign up for activities based on notices in the parish bulletin (although it is *possible* that *some* of these people *can* be leaders). You're looking for *leaders*, that is, people who have *followers* whom they can bring into the social mission of the parish. When we ask groups of social ministry leaders to brainstorm the qualities of a leader, they name listening skills, communication skills, healthy anger, sense of humor, spirituality, awareness of death, and most important, "has followers."

A Relational Tool: The 1-1 Meeting

To learn if someone is a leader, and perhaps invite that person into deeper leadership commitments, you have to know his or her story. There is no better way to learn someone's story than the 1-1 relational meeting. If you've ever trained with one of the major community-organizing networks, you have probably heard this before.

The 1-1 relational meeting (or simply 1-1) is a thirty-minute conversation with another parishioner intended to develop a public relationship. Public relationship? A public relationship is a relationship based on shared values, leading to action on public issues; it is not the same as a friendship. Through the questions you ask, you learn a person's motivations, uncover talents, and gauge leadership potential. Ed Chambers, director of the Industrial Areas Foundation, first developed the systematic use of 1-1s in community organizing. Here's how he describes the discipline:

> The relational meeting is a thirty- to thirty-five-minute opportunity to set aside the daily pressures of family, work, and deadlines to focus deliberately upon another person, to seek out their talent, interest, energy, and vision....No matter how interesting it is, don't violate the thirty-minute rule. In a relational meeting, you're checking people out, piquing their curiosity, and looking for talent, not for friends or "dialogue." Time discipline will help you keep focussed on public business. If the first thirty minutes goes well, don't keep going—schedule another meeting....The relational meeting is an art form that forces you to work within a time frame. Something in the nature of these meetings requires discipline about time. These are moments of intensity that cannot be sustained.[4]

In a moment of intensity, a 1-1 may indeed cover topics of emotional weight, but it is not therapy. Neither is it an intrusion into people's lives or a bit of coffee hour chitchat. It is not a survey, and you are not selling anything. *That* would be a return to Bertha's instrumental methods.

How do you learn what "makes a person tick" in a half-hour? The answer is relentless questioning, along with selective self-disclosure. I like to spend two-thirds of the time asking questions about the other person, such as:

- What do you think of your neighborhood? How has it changed over time? What is your vision for the area?

- What has your experience of the parish been like? What would be the ideal?
- Why did you do that? (This question follows after people share, as they inevitably will, some decision that they have made: to go back to school, to move to another city, to join an organization, and so on.)
- Who have been your heroes? your mentors?
- What gets you angry?
- Who are some other people in the parish with whom I should meet?

I typically ask questions about family, and if the person has children, I ask about the challenges of raising children. I share some of my own story, but I always make sure that the person speaks twice as much as I do. The meeting is usually in the person's home or at the parish.

One of the most important lessons I have learned is to trust my instincts. What clues do potential leaders offer about themselves? What am I curious about that I should follow up on?

With whom do you meet? The best place to start is with the pastor. What makes him tick? You might be surprised. Pastors tell me all the time (gratefully), "You are the only person who ever asked me why I became a priest." After the pastor, think about key people in the parish—staff, of course, but also other key decision-makers in the parish. Don't make the mistake of running to the parish council first. Are the council members really the key decision-makers? In one parish I discovered that the most powerful layperson in the parish was not the parish council president but the person who chaired the bingo committee. In another parish it was the custodian of thirty-five years. Reflect on that old community organizing maxim (there are a lot of them in organizing): A leader is someone who has followers. Who has followers in your parish? They are the people whom you want involved in your social concerns committee. They needn't (and shouldn't) be overcommitted church committee leaders, just people to whom others listen. Pay particular attention to racial/ethnic groups and subcultures of the parish that are under-represented in other parish activities. Think creatively.

One workshop participant recently suggested outreach to young adults with tattoos.

How do you set up the 1-1? A great question. Some people don't respond well to the cold call: "Hi, I'm Jeff, and I'd like to get to know you better." "No thanks, weirdo!" A more effective approach is to telephone people with whom you would like to explore leadership possibilities and offer an endorsement from someone whom they trust. "Hi, I'm Jeff. I work with the social concerns committee at St. Ann's. Msgr. Boyle said that you'd be a good person to talk to. I'd like thirty minutes of your time, in the next couple of weeks, to discuss some of your thoughts about our parish and community." Don't do the meeting over the phone, and make sure that you set a specific appointment.

How do you know if someone is a leader? I like to do two written evaluations after a 1-1, first of myself, then of the other person's leadership potential. I ask questions like these:

- Did I get beyond generalities and chitchat? Do I now know something of what makes this person tick?
- What do I need more information about?
- Did I get new leads, suggestions of other people to meet with? Which of these people do I want to arrange meetings with?
- What would I do differently next time?

Then I shift gears and evaluate the person's potential as a leader:

- What do I remember about this person?
- What gifts does he or she bring to the table?
- Do I like this person?
- Does he or she have values, hope, vision, or experiences that would add to the social concerns committee?
- Did the person show curiosity and ask me questions?

If my answers to the latter set of questions are encouraging, I try to schedule a second meeting with the leader. Rarely have I been turned down. Quite the opposite. People say, "During the twenty years that I've been going to this church, no one ever asked me what I thought about it!"

Using 1-1s to Identify and Develop Leaders

I once heard a board game described as taking a minute to learn and a lifetime to master. You could look at 1-1s that way. What could be simpler than talking to people for thirty minutes about their life? But it takes practice to learn the most helpful questions to ask and to discern the right leaders.

If I had not done effective 1-1s, I never would have challenged Paula Snow's assertion that she was "just a cafeteria lady." Paula was a secondary leader in the Brockton Interfaith Community. Paula riveted my attention during our fourth meeting. She said that during the twelve years that she served lunch to the schoolchildren of Brockton, seven of those children had been murdered before their twentieth birthday. This slight woman's hands shook with anger as she talked. "We've got to do something for these kids before another one is killed," she said.

As Paula spoke, I remembered the affection that we had for the cafeteria ladies in my own elementary school. I realized that for many of them, it was more than a job; they felt a vocation to work with children. Paula also shared with me her experience of invisibility within the school: "The principal runs the school. The teachers run the classroom. The secretaries have the dirt on everybody. And the janitor has the keys to every room. I'm invisible."

Anger. I felt a righteous anger in Paula. Anger that the innocent children she fed grew up into gang-bangers and dead bystanders. Anger at her own invisibility in a school system that ignored her gifts and passion for children. What could she do with this anger? Together with her parishioners and the congregants of sixteen other churches and synagogues, we would find out. I asked Paula to become a primary leader in a campaign to rid Brockton of youth violence. If I had not met with her three other times, each time probing a bit deeper, she probably would not have shared this side of herself with me.

Jesus used 1-1s too. We know from scripture that Jesus asked tough questions and sometimes gave harsh advice, like "Let the dead bury their own dead" (Matt 8:22). All of the scriptural references to eating and drinking give some clues as to how he came to know his disciples—both their talents and their limitations. He took that knowledge of strengths and weaknesses, gifts and liabilities, and, after a whole night of prayer, invited the Twelve into a deeper level of leadership.

These invitations did not end with the naming of the apostles. Do you remember the story of Jesus walking on water (Matt 14:22–36)? This well-known scripture illustrates how Christ invites his disciples to make deeper commitments and to meet greater challenges. Imagine the setting: A large seaside gathering is breaking up, and Jesus sends the disciples ahead of him in a boat to the opposite shore. He spends the evening on a mountain in prayer as the disciples travel a few miles out to sea and encounter rough weather.

> And early in the morning he came walking towards them on the lake. But when the disciples saw him walking on the lake, they were terrified, saying, "It is a ghost!" And they cried out in fear. But immediately Jesus spoke to them and said, "Take heart, it is I; do not be afraid." Peter answered him, "Lord, if it is you, command me to come to you on the water." He said, "Come." So Peter got out of the boat, started walking on the water, and came towards Jesus. But when he noticed the strong wind, he became frightened, and beginning to sink, he cried out, "Lord, save me!" Jesus immediately reached out his hand and caught him.

You don't have to walk on water to build a community of salt and light. But if you want to be a leader in social ministry, you have to be able to challenge people as Christ did. Jesus knew that Peter needed a challenge. Indeed, Peter asked for it. Jesus encouraged Peter because he knew he had the capacity to meet the challenge. When Peter met the challenge only halfway, Jesus "reached out his hand and caught him."

I had a strong instinct to invite Paula to become a primary leader in Brockton Interfaith Community's youth violence campaign, but I had some unanswered questions. Could she stand up to her ultimate boss, Brockton's superintendent of schools? Could she channel her anger in a constructive way, what legendary Industrial Areas Foundation organizer Ernesto Cortes calls "cold anger"?[5] Could she transform herself from an invisible cafeteria lady to a powerful leader of a strong citizens' organization? As sure as I was that I wanted Paula to lead this campaign, I was also aware of these obstacles. I knew that in some ways it would have been easier for her to walk on water than to meet all three of these challenges. But Jesus lifted her up each time she started to sink. And Jesus asked me to help, in my own small way, with the tools that I had to offer. All that we did together was based on the relationship forged in 1-1s.

If you are a social ministry leader, you can do the same. You *must* do the same. I'm talkin' about JESUS! Jesus got inside disciples' heads and learned what made them tick. He understood the challenges that they needed and issued those challenges, even when it meant that some people would become "quite sad." Remember the rich official in Luke? He asks Jesus what he must do to inherit eternal life. Jesus refers him to the commandments, but the man pushes back, insisting, "I have kept all these since my youth." When Jesus heard this, he said to him, "There is still one thing lacking. Sell all that you own and distribute the money to the poor, and you will have treasure in heaven; then come, follow me." Jesus issues a challenge based in his relationship with the official. Is the man up to it? The scripture continues, "But when he heard this, he became sad; for he was very rich" (Luke 18:18–23).

In this passage Jesus issues a challenge based on his relationship with the would-be disciple, but the official does not rise to the challenge. This will happen to you, too. The best organizers don't take it personally or try to talk people into taking on a challenge that they are not ready to meet. A good organizer simply moves on and continues talking with others, building more relationships and inviting more leaders to meet greater challenges. So, give the relational methods of Jesus a chance. How about doing five 1-1s during the next month? In the end, I guarantee, your efforts will look more like Jesus' miracle of the loaves and fishes than Bertha's Last Judgment.

The Social Concerns
Committee That Works

A relational approach builds a community of salt and light. Just ask
Sr. Christine Dobrowolski, IHM, director of social ministries at the
Church of the Epiphany in Louisville, Kentucky. Sixty parish leaders serve on subcommittees of the larger social-responsibility committee of the parish. Their task? To enlist the entire parish in the
social mission of the church through the various ministries that
parishioners have initiated. Sr. Dobrowolski explains that the structure of the parish's social ministries originated from *Communities of
Salt and Light* but then evolved into its current structure. The
social-responsibility committee includes groups of eight to twelve
parishioners who work to engage the parish in the following areas:

- environmental concerns
- prison ministry
- CLOUT (a community organizing project)
- hunger and poverty
- legislative advocacy
- Pax Christi
- Latino concerns
- undoing racism
- women's concerns
- twinning parish (El Salvador)
- twinning parish (Raymondsville, Texas)
- 10 percent group (10 percent of weekly parish income
  goes to the needy; for example, a small-grants program
  recently funded portable housing units for farm workers
  sleeping in stables)
- mediation and conflict resolution (facilitators of dialogue
  around difficult issues in the parish, such as the death
  penalty)

Social-responsibility committee members also encourage parishioners to serve on local boards and otherwise become active in civil
society. They provide input on the prayer and worship life of the

parish that Dobrowolski relates to the pastor and other staff at monthly meetings.

Relational models of leadership development abound at the Church of the Epiphany. Subcommittee chairs bring in new leaders by invitation, but also through a parish-wide stewardship process in which parishioners discern their own gifts and pledge them to the parish. In addition, newcomers attend a quarterly brunch in which interests and gifts surface in both structured and unstructured conversations. Attention to leadership development does not end with the invitation to action. Each subcommittee meeting includes prayer, education, and action, elements that will "stretch them," as Dobrowolski puts it. Her insistence on "stretching" leaders also extends to an annual retreat and other formation opportunities throughout the year. In addition, after a few years of service leaders are invited to move on to a new subcommittee. This keeps the subcommittees fresh and mitigates against single-issue approaches.

Whew! Are you exhausted? That sounds like a lot of work. I share this example just to show what can be done, outside of a bishops' statement of the ideal. Communities of salt and light do exist. The Church of the Epiphany is just one. But where do you start? Sr. Dobrowolski offers some sage advice for those seeking to build a community of salt and light: Take one step at a time.

PART II

Conversion: *"My Lord and My God!"*

2

The JustFaith Phenomenon

In JustFaith I met Jesus. In the faces of the poor, I met Jesus.
In the lives of courageous women and men fighting for peace
and justice, I met Jesus. In the struggles of my companion
classmates, I met Jesus. And, like everyone who ever met
Jesus, I am changed now.

— Ed Cortas,
JustFaith graduate,
London, Kentucky

Jesus calls us out of the middle pew not only through *invitation*
(Chapter 1) but also through *conversion* and *empowerment*.
Conversion, the second of Jesus' three tools for engaging the middle
pew, is the focus of Chapters 2 through 5. Conversion-based formation programs utilize Jesus' relational methods to lead middle-
and upper-income Catholics out of the middle pew and into action
for justice. Through these experiences Christ meets us, face to face,
in the eyes of the hungry, the homeless, the broken. They are, as
Mother Teresa proclaimed, "Jesus in disguise." Effective conversion-
based formation programs bring disciples before the Christ of
Matthew 25. Like Thomas, these followers of Christ cry out "My
Lord and my God!" They are no longer doubting; their beliefs, priorities, and behaviors are transformed. The impossible becomes
plausible; out of despair blossom new relationships, and true sight
returns to the blind.

In this chapter we explore JustFaith, a social justice formation
program that consistently draws new leaders into the church's
social mission. We listen to JustFaith graduates' reflections on their

conversion experiences. We take a careful inventory of the JustFaith process and examine why it fosters compassion and conversion. Finally, we draw out lessons for engaging the middle pew applicable to the whole of Catholic social ministry. We begin with the testimony that opens this chapter.

Out of the Tomb

Ed Cortas and the apostle Thomas have something in common. They both placed their hands in Jesus' side and were forever transformed. A former systems analyst for General Electric, Cortas was one of the first of ten thousand Catholics to experience JustFaith, a thirty-week small-group exploration of the church's social mission, promoted first by Catholic Charities, USA, and now jointly promoted by CCUSA, Catholic Relief Services, and CCHD. Cortas recently joined the JustFaith staff after a few years as a community organizer in eastern Kentucky. He compares himself to other characters in the gospels when interpreting his JustFaith experience:

> Like the blind man, Jesus has opened my eyes to the poverty and violence that makes up the lives of so many of my sisters and brothers. Like the rich young man, I have heard Jesus' call to live radically and am frustrated and saddened by my inability to shed wealth and power. Like the Pharisee, Jesus' condemnation of my deadly adherence to empty spirituality rings in my ears. Like the deaf and dumb man, Jesus has opened my ears to hear the Gospel anew and given me courage to share its challenging message. Like Lazarus, Jesus has called me out of the tomb of my lifeless faith into the light of new life in him.[1]

Each JustFaith graduate describes his or her experience differently, but a common thread, *conversion*, binds together the testimonies.

Most JustFaith graduates echo Cortas's sentiments, employing language like "transformation," "radical change," and "conversion." To the uninitiated, it can be perplexing. What are these people so excited about, and why? What exactly happened in these groups? Simply put, JustFaith graduates have placed their hand in Jesus' side, and, like Thomas, they will never be the same.

Four Varieties of Conversion

Each participant comes to JustFaith with a different story, a particular world view, a unique faith journey. But JustFaith graduates utilize a common vocabulary of conversion to describe their experience. Extensive interviews with JustFaith participants, facilitators, and staff throughout the country have led me to discern four types, or categories, of JustFaith conversions. First, there is the Catholic with no previous involvement in social ministry who transforms into a social justice dynamo. Second is the disciple who has been active in direct service ministries (food pantries, clothes closets, and so on) but not social-change ministries (legislative advocacy, community organizing, and the like), who finds a new calling in social action. Third is the tired or discouraged social activist who becomes re-energized by participating in JustFaith. Fourth is possibly the most intriguing type. A small number of Catholics suspicious of or hostile to the church's social mission enlist. Much to their surprise, they too find themselves transformed.

Clarice Stuart, a JustFaith participant from Lafayette, Louisiana, shares a common experience of the first variety, the previously uninvolved Catholic:

> A year and a half ago, if you would have told me, "Clarice, you're going to be involved in all of these social justice activities," I would have said, "There's no way! I don't have the time or the energy!" What's different in me now is the commitment. I view things differently. I see the poor and the vulnerable and their needs in a different light. I had a conversion. Before, I always thought that I didn't have the time. Now we go to Baton Rouge to meet with our legislators and voice our opinions. I never would have done that before. Never! I'm not political.[2]

Stuart represents hundreds of JustFaith participants who walk out of the middle pew with little involvement or experience in social ministry.

Others, like Tim McCarthy, a counselor in Virginia Beach, Virginia, expand their commitments to embrace social action after completing JustFaith. McCarthy recalls how JustFaith moved him to work on the underlying causes of injustice:

> JustFaith made me step into the justice realm. I still run a family-counseling center, but I see myself letting go of more and more of that work and giving my time to efforts for justice. I am now very active in our local community action group, working on affordable housing. I'd say that there's not a day that passes when I'm not involved in that endeavor in some way.
>
> Through my participation in JustFaith, I've also made the decision to go to Haiti to be connected to parishes twinning with ours and become an advocate for the people in Haiti. The group of us who traveled to Haiti went to the US Embassy to advocate for the concerns that we had. We ended up going to the State Department and meeting with the person in charge of Caribbean affairs. It's not like I wasn't on this journey before, but JustFaith has added more of a focus, more of an intentionally.[3]

Maxine Hake of Winona, Minnesota, offers a similar recollection, but her story concerns the refueling of her commitment to social justice. A Catholic drawn to the social mission but frustrated with her parish's moribund social concerns committee, she signed up for JustFaith when someone she trusted recommended the experience. She recalls:

> JustFaith gave me a sense of optimism and energy. I think that there is an energy that is generated by a community built by people who come together to study and pray about justice. And that's what was lacking for me. More than the information, I was lacking the energy.

And in that sense of connection within your group and with all of the other JustFaith groups, you feel that you're not alone.[4]

The fourth type of JustFaith conversion is the individual who joins a group with a skeptical or even hostile attitude toward the church's social mission. Sr. Patricia Lamb of Grand Rapids, Michigan, a JustFaith facilitator, relates a not uncommon story:

> Last year, a particular gentleman signed up and I thought, "Oh, he's going to be trouble. He's very conservative and he's not going to listen to a thing that's being said." And then I thought, "Well, he'll just have to be open and listen to the spirit." Three or four classes into the session, in front of the whole group he said, "I cannot explain what has happened to me; I have had a complete conversion. I am not the same person who walked in this room. I am now beginning to see the problems in our world today, the causes of problems, the injustices. And I will never be the same."[5]

An isolated anecdote? Fr. Tim Taugher of Binghamton, New York, would disagree. He shares much the same story, about a JustFaith participant in his parish:

> A couple signed up, Francis and June Clark. I knew Francis's sister Marion from her work here with Citizen Action. Marion and Francis are like night and day on social action and justice issues. Francis thought that Marion was really "out there." And she couldn't believe that her brother was in this group. He stuck with it.
> Francis and June and I met after Christmas, and June said that they had just gone to buy sneakers. They usually just went into the store, bought the sneakers, and came out. This time Francis was looking at all of the labels, wondering if he should buy any. He never had that kind of struggle of conscience. That was in December. When we finished with JustFaith, he was working with Marion at Citizen Action on a municipal

living-wage campaign. He volunteered to write the living-wage proposal.[6]

Each of these participants represents hundreds of others who have completed JustFaith. Some move from little or no activity in social ministry to action in behalf of justice, others from direct service work or an experience of burnout to a fiery passion for justice, others from suspicion to embracing the church's social mission. JustFaith facilitators estimate that 75 to 100 percent of JustFaith participants experience one of these varieties of conversion. Christine Breu, associate director of JustFaith, puts the figure at 85 percent.

Conversion and Lifestyle

To be sure, these conversion experiences have led thousands of Catholics out of the middle pew and into the public arena. But JustFaith has also led many middle- and upper-income Catholics to question their consumer choices and to adopt a simpler lifestyle. Tom Walsh of San Jose, California, relates a common experience:

> I've been in the process of radically changing the way I live. The nine months that we went through JustFaith opened my eyes to how our world is and what I could do about it. It was like I had known this all my life and had never faced it, and now it was impossible not to face it. It was exhilarating.
>
> In order to change anything at all, I had to start by changing the way I live my life. We now try to live more simply. As a result, our expenses are five hundred dollars a month less. The savings goes to Bread for the World and Catholic Charities. We cut our food budget by 40 percent. We cut our clothing budget by 50 percent, entertainment by 80 percent. We eliminated 80 percent of our magazine subscriptions, We used to do some kind of entertainment twice a week; now we do volunteer work instead.[7]

Walsh's experience is representative of hundreds of JustFaith participants who simplify their lives after an experience of conversion. Lucio Caruso of Grand Rapids, Michigan, a group facilitator and now social action director for the diocese, observed a strong current of discussion about lifestyle and consumer choices in his group. He says:

> Everyone in our group was beginning to raise questions about their own lifestyle, suggesting, "Maybe we don't need all of this." One person was beginning to ask if he needed the size home he had. You could tell that this was a big struggle for him, and I wondered how his family would react to some of these new ideas. We began to ask questions about the human price of our own lifestyle. Questions like, "What wages do the people who produce the things we buy get?" We never put that together before JustFaith.[8]

So, what happened to these people? Why did they rise from the middle pew and march to the front lines of social action? How did they change from fairly average middle- and upper-income consumers to the kind of shoppers who check sneaker labels? All fair questions, to which the short answer is, I'm talkin' about JESUS! To understand the lessons that JustFaith has to teach us about engaging the middle pew, we must put ourselves in the participants' shoes. We now examine the architecture of the program itself, noting the content of the books, videos, "border crossings," and retreats in this thirty-week encounter with Jesus, as participants experienced it in 2003–4. In the remainder of this chapter we explore why JustFaith elicits such strong conversion experiences and lift up the lessons JustFaith has to teach all of us seeking to engage new leaders in social ministry.

The Architecture of JustFaith

Interviews with JustFaith facilitators and participants make it clear that the conversion experiences described above are a natural outcome of these groups. But why? To begin to answer this question, we need to understand the experience of participating in a JustFaith group. In 2003–4, each group read thirteen books, watched sixteen videos, met four times with people living in poverty, participated in two retreats intended to foster reflection on their faith journey, and experienced a global "village banking" simulation. The groups met weekly, in two-and-a-half-hour sessions, for thirty weeks, discussing each of these resources and experiences at length.

Books Read (in Chronological Order)

1. *Compassion: A Reflection on Christian Life.* Henri J. M. Nouwen, Donald P. McNeil, and Douglas A. Morrison. New York: Random House, 1983. Nouwen and the other authors of this book place compassion at the center of what it means to be a Christian, suggesting that compassion is an expression of God's love for us and our love for God.

2. *Opting for the Poor: A Challenge to North Americans.* Peter J. Henriot, SJ. Washington, DC: Center of Concern, 2004. This revised and updated edition offers advice about how to serve for and with the poor, practically and with compassion.

3. *Amazing Grace: The Lives of Children and the Conscience of a Nation.* Jonathon Kozol. San Francisco: Harper Collins, 1996. Jonathan Kozol describes the resilience of black and Hispanic children in the South Bronx, interweaving the stories of concerned parents, teachers, religious leaders, gang members, and people with HIV/AIDS.

4. *A Place at the Table: A Catholic Recommitment to Overcome Poverty and to Respect the Dignity of All God's Children.* United States Conference of Catholic Bishops. Washington, DC: USCCB Publishing, 2002. This statement of the United States Catholic bishops recommits the church to eradicating poverty through works of justice and charity.

5. *Eight Spiritual Heroes: Their Search for God.* Brennan Hill. Cincinnati: St. Anthony Messenger Press, 2002. Hill profiles eight individuals and their search for a particular aspect of God, for example, "Dorothy Day and the God of the Homeless," "Martin Luther King, Jr., and the God of the Mountain," and "Edith Stein and the God of the Cross."

6. *Dismantling Racism: The Continuing Challenge to White America*. Joseph Brandt. Minneapolis: Augsburg Fortress, 1991. This book challenges white Americans to look closely at racism in the United States and its location in individual attitudes and behaviors and in public systems, institutions, and culture.

7. *How Much Is Enough: Hungering for God in an Affluent Culture*. Arthur Simon. Grand Rapids, MI: Baker Books, 2003. Arthur Simon diagnoses America as suffering from "affluenza," or runaway materialism, and argues that money becomes an object of worship when passion for material things is stronger than compassion for the poor.

8. *No Room at the Table: Earth's Most Vulnerable Children*. Donald H. Dunson. Maryknoll, NY: Orbis Books, 2003. Personal stories of children living in developing countries support the author's contention that "humanity's real weapons of mass destruction are hunger, preventable disease, and indifference."

9. *Unexpected News: Reading the Bible with Third World Eyes*. Robert McAfee Brown. Philadephia: The Westminster Press, 1984. Robert McAfee Brown makes the case that Christians in the developing world interpret scripture differently from Christians in industrialized nations, providing a wealth of illuminating examples.

10. *Credible Signs of Christ Alive: Case Studies from the Catholic Campaign for Human Development*. John P. Hogan. New York: Rowman and Littlefield, 2003. Stories of low-income people developing power through organizations funded by CCHD stand alongside key quotes from Catholic social teaching in this uplifting collection.

11. *The Powers That Be: Theology for a New Millennium*. Walter Wink. New York: Doubleday, 1998. This book combines elements of Wink's acclaimed trilogy on "the Powers" to take on questions of good and evil within systems, institutions, and structures.

12. *Parish Social Ministry: Strategies for Success*. Tom Ulrich. South Bend, IN: Ave Maria Press, 2001. Tom Ulrich provides advice and tools for Catholics interested in starting or

reinvigorating social ministries in their parish in this read-
able book.

13. *Broken Bread, Broken Bodies: The Lord's Supper and World
Hunger.* Joseph Grassi. Maryknoll, NY: Orbis Books, 2004.
In this revision of the 1985 edition, Joseph Grassi describes
the connections between the broken bread of Eucharist and
the broken bodies of the hungry around the world.

Videos Watched (in Chronological Order)

1. *When Did I See You Hungry?* (37 min.). Burbank, CA: San
Damiano Foundation, 2002. Narrated by Martin Sheen,
this film presents mostly black-and-white still photographs
of people living in poverty, along with the photographer's
insights into faith and the poor.

2. *Marketplace Prophets: Voices for Justice in 20th Century* (60
min.). Washington, DC: USCCB Publishing, 1991. This
video, produced by the United States bishops, reviews a
century of Catholic social teaching.

3. *Business of Hunger* (28 min.). Maryknoll, NY: Maryknoll
World Productions, 1984. This film examines the devastating effect of cash-crop economies on the populations of
developing nations.

4. *In the Footsteps of Jesus* (segment I, 9 min.). Washington,
DC: USCCB Publishing, 2003. Providing an introduction
to the seven themes of Catholic social teaching, this video
also exhorts Catholics to answer the question, How does
God call you to make a difference in the world?

5. *Among the People: Facing Poverty in America* (53 min.).
Washington, DC: USCCB Publishing, 2002. Originally
broadcast on the Hallmark Channel and some NBC affiliates, this documentary shows how CCHD helps impover-
ished communities in the United States break free of cycles
of poverty through community organizing and economic
development.

6. *Portrait of a Radical: The Jesus Movement* (50 min.).
Westport, CT: Four Seasons Productions, 1990. This video
combines art work, music, and the reflections of Rev.

Richard Rohr, OFM, and others to explore the radical, dynamic, and passionate message of Jesus.

7. *The Shadow of Hate* (40 min.). Montgomery, AL: Southern Poverty Law Center, 1994. This Oscar-winning film chronicles episodes of intolerance throughout US history, from the plight of Quakers in colonial New England to the 1991 riots in Crown Heights, Brooklyn.

8. *Holy Pictures* (28 min. segment). Los Angeles: San Damiano Foundation, 2003. *Holy Pictures* stresses the importance of stillness and silence in spiritual practice, using black-and-white images of quiet spaces to evoke healing calm.

9. *Escape from Affluenza* (56 min.). Oley, PA: Bullfrog Films, 1998. This video suggests that audiences declare their independence from rampant consumerism and materialism by adopting simple living practices.

10. *Global Village or Global Pillage* (27 min.). Jeremy Brecher and Tim Costello. Boston: South End Press, 1998. Narrated by Ed Asner, this film indicates constructive ways that ordinary people around the world are addressing the impact of globalization on their communities, work places, and environments.

11. *SOA: Guns and Greed* (20 min.). Maryknoll, NY: Maryknoll World Productions, 2000. This video makes the case that the US School of the Americas trains foreign military leaders to protect the interests of large corporations and global financial institutions through the use of force in their home countries.

12. *Romero* (105 min.). Pacific Palisades, CA: Paulist Productions, 1989. This full-length feature film chronicles the transformation of Archbishop Oscar Romero from an apolitical, bookish priest to an inspired leader of the Salvadoran people.

13. *Holding Ground: The Rebirth of Dudley Street* (58 min.). Hohokus, NJ: New Day Films, 1997. Through the voices of residents, community activists, and city officials, this documentary shows how a Boston neighborhood was able to create and carry out its own agenda for change.

14. *Arms for the Poor* (25 minutes). Maryknoll, NY: Maryknoll World Productions, 1998. In this film Oscar Arias, Rep.

Cynthia McKinney, the Dalai Lama, and specialists in tracking the arms trade build a dramatic case against the US weapons-export business to developing countries.

15. *Gandhi* (45 min. segment). London: Goldcrest Films International, 1982. The 1982 Oscar winner for best picture chronicles the life of the Mohandas K. Gandhi, a lawyer who became the famed leader of the nonviolent Indian revolts against the British.

16. *The Man Who Planted Trees* (30 min.). White River Junction, VT: Chelsea Green, 1995. This Oscar-winning animated film retells the story of a simple man who possesses an innate feel for nature and creates a forest in a desolate, arid area.

Experiential Learning

- *Opening Retreat:* The opening retreat elicits a sharing of participants' faith journeys, life stories, and current struggles.

- *Border Crossings:* These four evening and/or Saturday morning experiences bring participants face to face with people living in poverty. For example, a border crossing might include a visit to a soup kitchen to meet homeless people and talk to organizers of a living-wage campaign. One of these border crossings is a modified CCHD Journey to Justice retreat (see Chapter 3).

- *CRS Microfinance Simulation:* Catholic Relief Services developed this simulation game to illustrate the effects of church programs providing small amounts of credit in poor areas of developing countries. Each participant is provided with a case study and roles. Together, the group simulates the experience of running a village bank for a (simulated) period of two months.

- *Closing Retreat:* During the closing retreat participants look back on the year and how JustFaith has affected their faith life, with special attention paid to the call that participants now hear as the program concludes.

Compassion and Conversion

Are you exhausted yet? Who in their right mind would sign up for such a grueling reflection on human misery? A lot of new leaders, that's who! Over ten thousand Catholics nationwide have completed JustFaith, and that number continues to grow. According to JustFaith facilitators, some enlist because a person they trust recommends the program, others join after attending an information session with Jack Jezreel, founder of JustFaith, whose provocative reflections provide a taste of what's to come. A few appear out of nowhere, responding to the church bulletin notice. A small number attend with spouses, drawn by the appeal of a church activity that couples can share. In short, different methods reach different people, with relational approaches dominating. The result is diverse groups of middle- and upper-income Catholics drawn from the middle pew who seek to deepen their faith through a collective immersion in the social mission of the church.

JustFaith founder and director Jack Jezreel explains that significant numbers of Catholics sign up for this demanding formation program because:

> God has made us with an appetite or an inclination to be connected to each other. When we talk about the work of social ministry or social action, essentially what we are talking about is how we are about each other's care. What we call social ministry or social action or justice or charity are expressions of what it means to be connected to each other, and that's how we are made. My claim is that we have a script in our cells crafted by God that says "I am making you in a way that you will be most satisfied and most fulfilled when you are a part of a community that takes very seriously its commonness and its solidarity.[9]

Jezreel believes in a natural-law hypothesis: humans are "hard wired" to seek communities of care, compassion, and solidarity. This notion provides the philosophical underpinnings for the entire project. Jezreel suggests that this drive for compassion and

solidarity motivates us because we are images of God. We are
drawn into the lives of the suffering just as God is drawn into
human history in response to the suffering of the Jews in Exodus.
He explains:

> We find ourselves drawn into places where human
> beings struggle and hurt and suffer because that's just the
> way we are made. My experience is that when we provide
> opportunities for people to sit side by side with those
> who have really suffered, those encounters are just plain
> life changing. Part of our task in social ministry is there-
> fore putting people in situations where they can be
> moved by those experiences. We have to get people out
> of their comfort zones.
>
> We tend to think about that psychologically or spiri-
> tually, but I think we also need to think about it geo-
> graphically and physically. There are a lot of people in
> parishes who come from very comfortable environ-
> ments. Those environments are deliberately structured
> by our society so that they don't see; they don't have to
> take in a lot of human suffering. Part of our task is to
> bridge some of those gaps.[10]

We can understand the JustFaith experience better if we see every
book, every video, and every border-crossing experience as
intended to awaken that human tendency toward compassion and
solidarity. Take a second look at the section above. Imagine yourself reading each book, watching each video, making each border
crossing with a group of fourteen other committed Catholics, each
seeking to live the faith more deeply. How could you *not* be transformed?

Jack Jezreel speaks of "getting people out of their comfort
zones." However, it is striking how much comfort JustFaith graduates find when they leave those "comfort zones." A significant
number of these middle- and upper-income Catholics sell large
homes and move into more modest houses, as literal a rejection of
a "comfort zone" as one could imagine. Earlier, Tom Walsh
described the process as "exhilarating." That doesn't conjure the

image of a dour, self-flagellating, grim do-gooder.[11] Walsh sounds like someone who has encountered the living Christ, someone who, like Thomas, has placed his hands in Jesus' side, touched the nail marks, and exclaimed, "My Lord and my God!"

How does JustFaith agitate and comfort simultaneously? Lucio Caruso, diocesan peace-and-justice director for the Diocese of Grand Rapids was, until his JustFaith experience, an adult formation director for a parish in Grand Rapids. He reflects on the JustFaith process through the discipline of adult formation:

> What I saw was truly formation, more than just education about issues or information. It involved a certain amount of information gathering, a certain amount of reading that brings awareness, but also *personalization* through the real stories in the books and the videos. You can't leave an image of children with a parent searching through garbage with all the dangers inherent in that without saying "Omigosh, this is not something just out there somewhere!" That happened to everyone. The other part of this "aha" or awareness was realizing that conversion was happening among others in the group. When questions of justice are engaged in a small community setting, that's some of the best stuff of formation.[12]

Caruso insists that the length of the JustFaith process helps bring about these conversions and life changes. Thirty weeks provides enough time to understand information about social justice issues, process feelings, and reflect on spirituality, theology, and scripture readings. This extended period also allows tough questions to be raised and answered.

The Tyranny of Small Expectations

Many pastoral ministers have questioned whether one person in their parish would sign up for such a demanding program, let alone a group of fifteen. Catholics are simply too busy, they reason, especially middle- and upper-income Catholics. JustFaith founder Jack Jezreel disagrees:

> There has been an assumption on the part of a lot of parish clergy and ministers that people are very busy. Therefore, if we are going to do anything in parishes, it has to be abbreviated, short and not very demanding. The thinking is, "If we are going to get people to our event, it can't be very big because people don't have that kind of time." I would call all of this "the tyranny of small expectations." When you dig a little deeper underneath how busy people are, you learn that part of the busyness is ten hours of watching television each week, two videos, and golf twice a week. Yes, people live busy lives, but they also prioritize. In addition, many Catholics have an intuitive sense that what God is drawing us into is not "small potatoes," not an insignificant commitment.[13]

Jezreel's experience is that asking a greater commitment of Catholics in the middle pew results in getting a greater commitment from them. Great commitments of time and energy may not be for everyone, but they have always been part of the church, through religious communities and lay movements such as Focolare, Opus Dei, and the Jesuit Volunteer Corps.

Steve Colecchi, former director of the Office for Justice and Peace of the Diocese of Richmond, was an initial skeptic who came to believe in Jezreel's view of the "tyranny of small expectations." When leaders of the diocese's Sowers of Justice organization in Tidewater, Virginia, approached him in 2000 about sponsoring JustFaith in the diocese, he responded cautiously:

> I asked them, "Do you really think people will do an every-week commitment, two retreats per year, several immersion experiences, and read ten or twelve books over the course of the year?" But they were persistent. You always want to trust local leaders and honor their initiative, so my final judgment was that if they really

wanted to try this, I owed it to them. I agreed to support JustFaith financially and get involved in the promotion. We agreed to do JustFaith in the Tidewater area as a pilot to see if it could work.[14]

Colecchi recalls that eighty-three people signed up in seven groups for that pilot year. Eighty completed the process. Three dropped out for reasons like relocation and family illness. "I was amazed at the amount of energy that was generated, and I was amazed at how JustFaith expanded the numbers of people involved in Tidewater Sowers of Justice that year," he reflects.

The next year JustFaith became a diocesan-wide program, drawing in 300 new leaders. The following year 250 additional parishioners signed up. As a result, Colecchi has seen significant increases in the number of leaders involved in diocesan social justice activities. He reports:

> Since we started doing JustFaith, we've doubled the number of people engaged in social justice work in the diocese. And that's a conservative estimate. I've noticed, for example, that our Catholic Advocacy Day at the capital went from 120–130 people attending to 270–280 people registered. That's a remarkable growth in two-year's time for an event that has had stable participation over the years.[15]

As counter-intuitive as it might seem to pastoral ministers accustomed to asking less of busy parishioners, Jezreel's "if you ask more, you get more" holds up. In diocese after diocese across the country social action directors who promote JustFaith have noted significant increases in the numbers of leaders from the middle pew involved in both parish and diocesan social justice activities. The experience of watching the development of these new leaders has led many social action leaders to reevaluate their assumptions about the middle pew and to reflect on the lessons of JustFaith.

Lessons of JustFaith

An obvious lesson of the program is simply: try JustFaith. If you want to form leaders hungry and thirsty for justice, bursting out of the middle pew with energy, try JustFaith in your parish. That said, other lessons can be drawn from the JustFaith phenomenon that have implications for the whole of social ministry. Seven emerge as primary:

1. *Maintain high expectations of parish leaders.* Jesus had high expectations of his disciples. You should too. I'm talkin' about JESUS! In truth, many Catholics in the middle pew are hungry for a challenge. To repeat Jezreel's analysis, "They have an intuitive sense that what God is drawing us into is not 'small potatoes,' not an insignificant commitment."[16] Not to invite these disciples into a deeper relationship with Jesus through the church's social ministries because *you* think that they may be too busy is to sell both Christ and your fellow Christians short.

2. *It's all about Jesus.* You've got to love the relentlessness of the JustFaith process. Again and again JustFaith brings disciples face to face with the Christ of Matthew 25. Ed Cortas suggested in the first lines of this chapter that every encounter with Jesus is life changing. One might miss Jesus the first time, and maybe the second or third time, but fifty times? Repeated encounters with Jesus promote a depth of relationship with Christ. Good social ministry should borrow this healthy repetition, introducing Catholics of the middle pew to the wounded Christ again and again within the context of reflection on scripture and church teaching.

3. *Solidarity precedes compassion.* The sequencing of JustFaith is no accident. First, participants attend an introspective retreat, sharing their faith journey, building group solidarity, and creating an openness and vulnerability for the discussions to come. Second, meditations on compassion, readings about real people living in poverty, videos that show the faces of the poor and their living conditions, and live meetings with people living in poverty enable partici-

pants to develop a personal relationship with the poor, ultimately strengthening their own relationship with Christ. The same sequence of formation can be utilized in other areas of social ministry, particularly as an adjunct to ministries of charity.

4. *Action follows compassion.* JustFaith is designed not to push participants into action before formation is completed. The reason for this delay is that the personal relationship with Christ and the poor that develops is what gives JustFaith graduates so much energy for action. Parishes that offer opportunities for action should integrate formation elements inspired by JustFaith into each of these vehicles. For example, if during Lent your parish participates in Catholic Relief Services' Operation Rice Bowl or Bread for the World's Offering of Letters, look for ways to put a face on the poor that the parish seeks to help. In addition, think of ways to connect those faces to Christ.

5. *Afflict the comfortable.* There's a saying attributed to Dorothy Day that good social ministry comforts the afflicted while afflicting the comfortable.[17] Certainly many affluent Catholics find the promises of our consumer society to be quite empty indeed. JustFaith helps them simplify their lives, becoming "poor in spirit," and finding comfort in a simpler lifestyle. But reflecting on one's lifestyle and relationship to consumerism remains an underdeveloped area of Catholic social ministry. JustFaith has proven that many Catholics find this reflection exhilarating and not simply an opportunity to experience guilt. Such reflection should become a priority for Catholic social ministry.

6. *Travel in packs.* Sociologists are fond of asking if an individual can make a difference. I always reply, "An individual *in community* can make a difference." I honestly do not believe that an individual alone can do much more than become angry and bitter. But, as anthropologist Margaret Mead said: "Never underestimate the power of a few committed people to change the world. Indeed, it is the only thing that ever has."[18] The JustFaith phenomenon underscores Mead's point. Once participants complete the program and enter

the action phase, they often refuse to stop meeting. Others find new communities of support and agitation through the social change activities they take on. Put simply, JustFaith reminds us once again that the support of a community of disciples is essential to the success of Catholic social action.

7. *Invite people to write their own story.* When observers try to explain why JustFaith works, they often focus entirely on the content of the books and videos. But the program would not work quite so well without the "bookend" retreats that focus on the faith development of the participants and the discussions about personal faith development that come up in the weekly meetings. The questions driving the retreats are simple: (1) What has been your faith journey before entering JustFaith? (2) How is your faith life different now? Good social ministry needs reflective moments. If we are to promote encounters with Jesus, we must also invest in helping disciples understand those encounters and their effect on the spiritual life.

Yet, even as JustFaith draws new leaders out of the middle pew and into the social mission of the church, it is also true that JustFaith is not for everyone. Nor is it the only way to engage new leaders. It might be exciting that JustFaith transforms the lives of fifteen or more individuals in the parish. Indeed, those fifteen or so disciples affect the lives of so many more through their witness and evangelization. But how do we reach the adults who are only ready for more modest experiences? And what about the youth of the parish? How do we provide them with developmentally appropriate encounters with the Christ of Matthew 25? How else can Catholics come face to face with Christ, crying out "My Lord and my God!" in a moment of conversion? These are the concerns at the heart of the next three chapters.

3

❖

A Journey to Justice

Jesus' *conversion* tool appears in several different applications. JustFaith is one. Another is Journey to Justice, a social justice formation retreat developed by CCHD. The Journey to Justice retreat brings affluent US Catholics from the middle pew face to face with Americans living in poverty. It is an increasingly rare opportunity for conversation between social classes in our stratified society, an experience that successfully engages new leaders in social ministry. In this chapter we take a comprehensive look at the Journey to Justice model, explaining how and why the retreat brings new leaders into Catholic social ministry, and offer universal lessons learned from studying the program. It is a conversion experience tantamount to dinner with the Lord himself, the topic of a much-loved youth-ministry skit passed down through oral tradition from one generation of teens to the next. One version of the skit follows.

My Dinner with Jesus

"Jesus is coming to dinner. Really. You mean he's never been to your house? Yes, he's coming. He called yesterday and said that he'd be over tonight for dinner. What should I make? Do you know if he's a vegetarian?"

"Wait, there's the doorbell. Yes?"

"You're hungry and you want something to eat? Sorry, I'm terribly busy. I have an important guest coming over!"

"Where were we? Oh yes, what to make Jesus for dinner. Oh! There's the bell again! Hi Joey, what are you doing here? Your parents had a big fight and you want to crash at my place? Well, I have a really important visitor coming over soon. Maybe you should try Miranda. I bet she's not busy."

"So anyway…he likes fish, right? Maybe I'll make fish. Oh, I can't believe this! The doorbell again! Hi Carla. No, Maristella isn't home. I'm sorry that you're lonely, but I don't have time to play. I have an important guest coming over."

"You know, Jesus was supposed to be here by now. I'm surprised that he's late. He's the Son of God, right? Do you think that if he was running late he could stop time or something and catch up? Wait, there's call waiting!"

"Oh, hi Jesus, what's up? I was expecting you a half-hour ago. What? You came to my house three times and I turned you away?"

My Lord and my God! My Lord and my God!

This popular youth-ministry skit illustrates the hubris of those who believe themselves devout but who would turn Jesus away at the door. People in need surround us, but we too often see them as stereotypes, symbols, or statistics, failing to recognize them for who they are: Jesus in disguise. Most Catholics need help in discerning Christ in the poor. But, as the JustFaith graduates profiled in Chapter 2 articulate so well, when middle- and upper-income Catholics encounter the poor and vulnerable in the context of learning about scripture and church teaching, the result can be transformative. New leaders arise from the middle pew and, with encouragement, become engaged in social ministry.

A Journey to Justice

Imagine for a moment that the protagonist in "My Dinner with Jesus" had spent the previous hours talking about stereotypes and concerns regarding the poor, studying the parable of the good Samaritan, and learning about Catholic social teaching. Would these experiences change the person's interactions with the needy at the door? You bet! Imagine further that those who knocked at the door were people living in poverty who had organized for change, altering existing power relationships to give low-income people a place at the table of public life. They come to the door not to ask for a handout, but to work in partnership with middle- and upper-income Catholics from the middle pew to build the kingdom of God (and maybe put up a stop sign on the corner of North and Main). These are the empowered poor.[1]

If you can envision this scene, you already have a good idea of how the Journey to Justice retreat works. CCHD developed the Journey to Justice program to facilitate structured encounters between empowered people living in poverty and wealthier Catholics. For twelve years CCHD has offered Journey to Justice retreats to middle and upper-income parishes and clusters of parishes.

Journey to Justice is one way that CCHD works both to educate and to engage the middle pew in the work of social justice. Through a combination of community building, teaching about scripture and Catholic social doctrine, social analysis, and an immersion experience with a CCHD-funded group, the retreat gives Catholics a direct experience of Jesus Christ in the empowered poor. Many participants become engaged in the church's social mission as a result.

The effects of the Journey to Justice retreat are not as lasting as a year-long experience like JustFaith or the global mission experiences and long-term service-learning commitments described in Chapters 4 and 5. The intensity of a weekend experience can be great, but a shepherd must be prepared to call "Follow me!" after participants cry out "My Lord and my God!" to help leaders take the next step on their journey to justice. For this reason CCHD requires a commitment to follow-up activities on the part of the sponsoring parish or cluster of parishes.

Three locations where Journey to Justice retreats have catalyzed the development of impressive social ministries are St. Aloysius Parish in Spokane, Washington; St. Joan of Arc Parish in Boca Raton, Florida; and the deaneries (clusters of parishes) of the Diocese of Davenport, Iowa. The results of these retreats and the local follow-up activities have important implications for us as we continue to examine how parish social ministry organizers can utilize conversion experiences to develop new social ministry leaders from the middle pew. First, let us look at the retreat structure.

The Architecture of Journey to Justice

Journey to Justice comprises a full weekend of activity, from Friday evening to Sunday at noon. Eight sequential sessions lead participants through a process that is both experiential and reflective.

1. *Preferential Option for and with the Poor (Friday):* The opening session sets the context for the retreat and explores the preferential option for the poor in Catholic social teaching and scripture. In small groups participants discuss their beliefs and feelings about people living in poverty, which initially can be quite negative.
2. *Entering Scripture (Saturday):* The parable of the good Samaritan provides an opportunity to explore the question Who is my neighbor? and examine the social meaning behind Jesus' choice of a Samaritan as the hero of the story.
3. *Common Ground and Immersion (Saturday):* This segment includes two parts. First, participants view the video *Breaking the Cycle of Poverty: Facing the Future with Hope,* which helps them prepare, mentally and emotionally, for dialogue with the low-income leaders. After some discussion of the video and the need to look for the story behind the story, retreatants meet with a CCHD-funded group for a tour and dialogue with empowered people living in poverty.
4. *What We've Seen and Heard (Saturday):* This session gives participants an opportunity to process their experience of meeting the empowered low-income group, sharing what they observed and felt during the immersion experience. They also begin to explore what they might gain, as well as give, in an ongoing relationship with the group.
5. *Sin and Grace (Saturday):* Saturday's immersion experience culminates with an evening discussion of social sin and its relationship to personal sin. Both the *Catechism of the Catholic Church* and Pope John Paul's 1984 letter "Reconciliation and Penance" figure prominently in this session.
6. *Social Analysis (Sunday):* The final day begins with a workshop on social analysis within the context of the pastoral circle (experience → social analysis → theological reflection

→ action).[2] Participants analyze the root causes of poverty, with particular reference to the issues faced by the CCHD-funded group.

7. *Imagining Anew (Sunday):* The seventh session leads participants through a guided imagery experience to stimulate creative responses to poverty and to the empowered low-income leaders.

8. *Commitment and Closing Liturgy (Sunday):* In the retreat's final session participants make a commitment to attending a follow-up meeting focused on action. The commitment (understood by participants when they sign up for the retreat) is made within a liturgical context: a Mass, a reconciliation service, or a prayer service.

CCHD education specialists insist that each step of the Journey to Justice process is essential, but I believe that two segments especially warrant further exploration.

The Good Samaritan (Session 2)

The presentation and dialogue on the parable of the good Samaritan (Luke 10:25–37) put Jesus' teachings on compassion, religious legalism, and racial justice center stage immediately prior to the immersion experience. I would argue that this is the most important formation exercise in the retreat. Why? I'm talkin' about JESUS! Studying the parable of the good Samaritan helps prepare the participants for their own "Dinner with Jesus."

You will remember the basics of the story: a scholar of the Law, or religious lawyer, approaches Jesus in Luke 10:25–37, asking, "What must I do to inherit everlasting life?" The lawyer seems to want to pigeonhole Jesus more than he wants to improve his spiritual life. It is not an entirely sincere question. Jesus wisely throws the query back at him. The lawyer replies:

> "You shall love the Lord your God with all your heart and with all your soul, and with all your strength, and with all your mind; and your neighbor as yourself." And [Jesus] said to him, "You have given the right answer; do

this, and you will live." But wanting to justify himself, he asked Jesus, "And who is my neighbor?"

The first attempt to trap Jesus didn't work, so the lawyer tries again, asking, "Who is my neighbor?" Jesus responds with the parable we know so well. A Levite, a priest, and a Samaritan all pass a wounded crime victim, abandoned for dead on the side of the road. The first two pass the victim by, prohibited by Jewish law from touching the "unclean" victim. The Samaritan comes next. He binds the man's wounds, takes him to an inn, and pays the innkeeper to care for the wounded man until he returns. Jesus asks the lawyer, "Who was a neighbor to the man?" The scholar correctly replies, "The one who showed him mercy."

Two lessons are contained in the parable. First, love and compassion are the supreme Law, but love brings with it certain obligations. Second, by making the Samaritan the hero of the story, Jesus is making a statement about race. Samaritans were members of a distinct ethnic group despised by the Jews of the day. Simply by telling the story, Jesus turns the social conventions of the time on their head. Indeed, he goes a step further in the parable, implying that one cannot determine who a neighbor is based on race.

The Journey to Justice facilitator's manual notes that Jesus also imparts the message, "Be prepared to abandon presuppositions." Think back to our young friend in "My Dinner with Jesus." Would reflection on the good Samaritan parable have helped that person? Indeed, discussing the scripture provides an ideal preparation for the retreatants own "Dinner with Jesus." The parable ultimately proves more powerful within the context of Journey to Justice than Matthew 25, because it raises the question, What does it mean to be neighbor? The empowered poor who meet with the Journey to Justice retreatants do not ask for a bite of food or a drink of water; they ask for a partnership, a new notion of being neighbor for those accustomed to offering only charity to the poor.

Meeting the Empowered Poor (Session 3)

The most crucial segment of the Journey to Justice retreat is without question the face-to-face meeting with the CCHD-funded group. All of the discussion of stereotypes of the poor, Catholic social teaching, and the reflection on the parable of the good Samaritan lead up to this encounter.

The format is simple. Participants leave the retreat site and travel to the headquarters of the organization or to the home of one of its members. They listen and learn about the life stories of the group's members, how the organization formed, its current activities, and some of the group's accomplishments. They ask questions. They get answers. And they share food. The empowered low-income leaders also suggest ways that the middle- and upper-income retreat participants could be neighbors to them. *Jesus is coming to dinner. Really.*

Rita Waldref, pastoral associate at St. Aloysius Parish in Spokane, Washington, describes a typical immersion experience:

> We invited Voices for Opportunity In Childcare, Education, and Support (VOICES) to meet with us. After the meeting, people were in tears, it was so profound. It's an immersion experience into a life that most of us don't know, being homeless and not having enough money for food. One person talked about living in a car. Participants met real people from Spokane who lived on the margins, people we often don't hear about.
>
> They talked about the challenges of living in poverty, but they talked about raising their voices to advocate. Through VOICES they learned how to speak and write as advocates, locally, statewide, and nationally. VOICES got more funds appropriated for social service groups in Spokane and they were successful in convincing the city to maintain bus routes in our public transportation system. They made us aware of how one situation, like transportation, can affect so many of the poor and those on the margins.[3]

Most Journey to Justice participants are moved by the dialogue with people living in poverty, but they also express surprise at what they learn about the accomplishments of the empowered (and organized) poor.

Anita Chlipala, a University of Iowa student, participated in a Journey to Justice retreat at the university's Newman Center. This retreat focused on the struggles of small family farmers driven into poverty by competition from giant factory farms. She reflects on the students' attitudes toward people living in poverty before and after the retreat:

> We had a lot of stereotypes and generalizations about the poor: they were powerless, they didn't have money, they might have been on welfare. Visually, we thought of the homeless. It was very enlightening when we met people who were dealing with the hog confinements, because it was a different aspect of poverty. They were so different from what we thought at the beginning of the retreat. The added element was that they were empowered and getting together to fight the hog confinement industry.[4]

John Hogan, author of *Credible Signs of Christ Alive: Case Studies from the Catholic Campaign for Human Development,* attended this Journey to Justice retreat while researching his book. Within that well-written and engaging book, Hogan documents the struggles of family hog farmers who were sliding ever more into poverty against the factory farms of the major hog producers. He offers a narrative description of the presentation that Chlipala and her peers heard:

> Peggy spoke about the horrible smell coming off the large hog confinements, especially during periods when manure is being spread. For at least two weeks a year, she cannot even go outside. She and her husband move to the basement. She packs her two teenage children off to their grandparents. The stench from the five hog sites around her farm as well as the "dead pig" storage facility is overpowering her and her family. Frank chimed in that the smell would "gag a maggot." Jodi sadly spoke of her neighbor, "he suffers from emphysema and is on oxygen....Every time one of the facilities spreads manure, he is driven from his home. The horrible stench and toxic

fumes coming from the facilities make him sicker than he already is. He can't breathe even with the oxygen.[5]

Chlipala noted that the students went into the retreat with lots of stereotypes about the poor. They left remarking how much the low-income leaders reminded them of their grandparents. Now that's a new view of neighbor!

Many Journey to Justice participants describe the direct encounter with people living in poverty as transformative. Marjorie O'Sullivan, a parishioner at St. Joan of Arc Parish in Boca Raton, Florida, compares the encounter to the meeting of Jesus and Zacchaeus, the tax collector. In Luke 19:1–10 Zacchaeus climbs a tree to get a better look at Jesus ("for he was short in stature"). Jesus notices the man, recognizes his status as tax collector (a high-income sinner), and says, "I must stay at your house today." Visibly moved by Jesus' outreach, Zacchaeus responds, "Half of my possessions, Lord, I will give to the poor; and if I have defrauded anyone of anything, I will pay back four times as much." Jesus replies, "Today salvation has come to this house." O'Sullivan believes that "what happened to Zacchaeus is what happens in Journey to Justice."[6] Zacchaeus therefore stands for all of the middle- and upper-income Catholics who have taken the retreat and walked away transformed by the encounter with Christ. *My Lord and my God!*

These two retreat segments, the reflection on the parable of the good Samaritan and the meeting with the empowered poor, are the two key movements of the retreat. They supply the energy that propels those attending out of the middle pew and into parish-based action for justice. At the beginning of this chapter I noted that the retreat by itself does not produce this outcome, that follow-up work is necessary to bring in significant numbers of new leaders. We turn now to the three locales where strong pastoral leadership harnessed the energy of Journey to Justice and engaged dozens of new leaders from the middle pew.

Transforming Individuals and Parishes

When Rita Waldref first heard about Journey to Justice, she recognized the retreat as the ideal springboard to launch a parish social justice committee at St. Aloysius Church in Spokane, Washington, where she served as a pastoral associate. She recruited thirty-seven parishioners to attend through a publicity campaign and personal invitations. A few weeks after the retreat she gathered the participants to discuss how the retreat had affected them and what next steps they wished to take. The group decided to form a social ministry committee, and over half of the leaders have stuck with it for the long haul.

Five years later the St. Aloysius social ministry committee has developed into a model of what it means to become a community of salt and light. In addition to several direct service ministries to the homeless, seniors, and the disabled, the committee now organizes:

- an election-year candidates' forum and twice-annual voter registration drives
- Catholic Relief Services' Operation Rice Bowl
- participation in the Washington Association of Churches legislative conference
- leadership in the Spokane Alliance community organization
- a nonviolent lifestyle educational group
- sales of Fair Trade coffee and Work of Human Hands crafts
- A JustFaith group[7]

The Journey to Justice retreats remain focal to the development of the social ministry committee. Waldref organizes one in the parish each year, changing the theme annually. For example, the most recent retreat featured a dialogue with a low-income group working on environmental justice. About half of those who participated in the first retreat have attended one or two more retreats from 1999 to 2004 and become involved in one or more projects of the parish social ministry committee. New leaders for the social ministry committee also emerge from these annual retreats. Waldref explains that the retreats attract new parish members who seek to become involved in the church in some way. They tend to see the Journey to Justice retreat as an interesting experience that will also help them get acquainted with others in the parish. Once they participate in the retreat, many are hooked, becoming leaders in the social ministry committee.

As was the case with JustFaith, the middle pew parishioners who enlist in Journey to Justice come from a variety of backgrounds. Some have prior involvement in social action but for various reasons have not acted on those commitments in years. Others have simply lived their lives without ever venturing into the public square. What they have in common is little or no previous involvement in parish social ministry.

One leader whose life was significantly changed by the initial Journey to Justice retreat is Kathleen Stephens, a disabled parishioner who had been disappointed by an earlier attempt to form a social ministry committee. She agreed to attend after a personal invitation from Waldref. She recounts the effects of the retreat on her attitudes toward herself and social ministry:

> When I was younger, I was going to save the world, and I was going to do it in a year's volunteer experience. I tried that a couple of times and it didn't work. I was fifty years old when I made the Journey to Justice retreat. My perspective had become, "Well, I'm not young anymore, and I can't tromp up and down the streets of an Indian reservation like I did when I was twenty-five, and there's not a lot of activity that I can do," which was wrong! I discovered that I have skills and talents and abilities, and one way I could use them was to be on the social justice committee.
>
> The retreat helped me see that I didn't need to focus on the things that I couldn't do because there was a huge amount that I could do that I hadn't realized. Even though I can't do all of the things that we plan because I'm fifty-seven, and I have fibromyalgia, osteoarthritis, and a full-time job, we've got a whole parish. One of our goals is that everyone in our parish experience some-

thing in the social justice realm once a year. By being on that planning team, I can use my skills and abilities well within my physical limitations.[8]

Stephens believes that it was hearing the stories of the low-income leaders working with their limitations that led her to realize how much she could do despite her own handicaps. Her spiritual life changed as well. She recalls:

> The Journey to Justice retreat made me feel more hopeful. I didn't see anything I hadn't seen before, but I started to see connections, and I started to see much more clearly how people work into God's plan. I'd always seen spirituality as a me-and-God thing. It's not how it is exactly; it's more of a God-and-us thing. A group of people can really get things done that God-and-I alone can't do because of my limitations. They're not really limitations from God's point of view because God expects me to get help. He doesn't expect me to do everything alone. I kind of knew that, but I didn't really know it. And now I *really* know it.[9]

On the social ministry committee, Stephens works on disability access issues. "Access is a lot bigger than putting 'curb cuts' on your sidewalk," she explains. "Access means that every person has the opportunity to lead a full and meaningful life. The term doesn't limit itself to people with disabilities, because people who have very low incomes lack access too, like to health care." Stephens's words suggest that Journey to Justice itself has helped her, as well, to live a more full and meaningful life.

In Boca Raton, Marjorie O'Sullivan worked with other lay leaders at St. Joan of Arc Parish to develop a new social ministry after the initial Journey to Justice retreat in the mid-1990s. They created an organization devoted to supporting CCHD-funded groups and working on local race relations. They also exported Journey to Justice to nearby parishes. O'Sullivan's first immersion experience, with an immigrant Haitian community organization, did not go as expected:

The conversation surprised us. They said "We don't want your clothes. We don't even want your money. We want your respect." This was a time when Haitians could not give blood because they were considered "contaminated." We processed the experience, and after dinner we had a presentation on social sin, to bring out the idea that evil can be incorporated into systems and structures. We can participate in sinful structures without even realizing that we are.[10]

Energized by the retreat, O'Sullivan and most of her fellow retreatants partnered with a Haitian community organization and began to discern specific projects to work on together.

Blessed with a number of accountants, the St. Joan of Arc parishioners led a Tax Return Fair with the Haitian organization for two Saturdays in the parish gymnasium. The accountants uncovered widespread improprieties as they completed the tax returns. Many of the Haitians, documented resident aliens, were employed as farm workers. Growers had systematically deducted taxes from their wages but had not paid the taxes to the government. The IRS then pursued the *workers* for nonpayment of taxes. The committee members contacted the IRS, and the growers were forced to pay the IRS.

Next, the St. Joan of Arc parishioners decided to work locally with African Americans, forming a dialogue group composed of black Baptists and white Catholics. The group met for scripture study and prayer, eventually taking action to persuade the city of Boca Raton to observe the Martin Luther King, Jr., holiday and to fund events commemorating Dr. King's birthday. The organization endured, taking the name DISC (Developing Interfaith Social Change) and continuing to promote interracial dialogue. DISC also began to draw new leaders from other parishes by bringing Journey to Justice retreats to the other Boca Raton parishes.

One of those parishes was St. Jude in Boca Raton. The immersion experience, led by O'Sullivan, focused on a migrant farm-worker organization. She recalls:

> The farm workers talked to us about their life and the injustice they experienced. They had to pay so much for food that we could purchase so much cheaper. How ironic! They were harvesting the vegetables! Their housing was awful. The people from St. Jude were so moved that they took up the issue of farm-worker housing. There were powerful, wealthy people in that group, including an architect and a construction contractor. They formed a housing corporation, and over time twenty-five families got decent, low-cost housing. They also taught literacy classes and ran a summer camp for the children.[11]

This housing corporation was the second new organization to result from the Boca Raton Journey to Justice retreats.

Journey to Justice made an impact on the lives of many in Boca Raton through the efforts of DISC; the spinoffs into other parishes, such as St. Jude's; and the work of other retreatants to develop community gardens and bring the citizenship development program That's Not Fair! into local elementary schools.[12] The experience also transformed individuals spiritually.

When O'Sullivan reflects on the changes in her life since becoming involved in Journey to Justice, she sounds a bit like Jesuit Volunteers who, with pride, call themselves "ruined for life":

> I am now permanently uncomfortable. And I know that I always will be. While I go about my comfortable, secure, middle-class life, people are struggling and dying. At first, that realization made me uncomfortable, and then I decided to just stay with the discomfort. It was the least I could do. It would not be right to be comfortable until they were. I would be uncomfortable but not despondent. Even though it sometimes seems that injustice is winning, there's always this force of struggle and people who are trying to help.[13]

Several other interviewees noted the same kind of discomfort. In the last chapter we described JustFaith's capacity to "afflict the comfortable." Journey to Justice retreats seem to have the same effect. The emphasis on developing relationships with *empowered* people living in poverty produces an emphasis on hope that coexists with the uncomfortable feelings that surface in the retreat and are internalized by many participants.

In the Diocese of Davenport that discomfort coalesced around issues of race. Nora Dvorak, a parish lay leader, notes:

> For many of the people who were at the Journey to Justice retreat, it was their first encounter with people of other races or ethnicities. Iowa is so white that people can go through their entire life without necessarily shaking hands, greeting, or saying hello to someone of another ethnic group. In this retreat they were in the same room; you came in touch with them, and you heard their stories about what it's like to be called the names that they hear because of their skin color.[14]

The experience led her deanery council to work on the issue of racial profiling after the retreat. Council members met with community leaders and local police to encourage police to track traffic stops of people of color in order to determine if they were being stopped excessively. Area police now collect such data and report directly to the group.

Another deanery held an urban Journey to Justice retreat in Davenport. The participants met with a low-income community organization in a leader's home. Jim Moran, a parishioner at Sacred Heart Cathedral, describes a tour of the house: "There was raw sewage in the basement," he recalls. "The woman had purchased the house from predatory lenders, who often turn roach-infested houses over to low-income buyers."[15] Working with the CCHD-funded community group, Moran and area parishioners took Davenport City Council members on tours of some of the homes in question. The result? Increased city home inspections to stop abusive home-selling practices. This victory turned out to be helpful to beleaguered renters as well, an unintended consequence.

The solidarity that developed between the parishioners and the empowered people living in poverty was one positive outcome of the Journey to Justice retreats. So were the victories on racial profiling and housing. But Journey to Justice also had a ripple effect on the structure of social ministry committee meetings in the Diocese of Davenport. Dan Ebener, social action director for the diocese, explains:

> Journey to Justice is now an ongoing part of what we do. It's not just a retreat. Our social action groups have made a decision to make theological reflection a major part of each meeting. After a brief prayer they read scripture and then discuss it, asking, "What is this saying to you?" People feel very nourished by this; they're being fed. Sometimes this will go for a half-hour. We've really retained leaders over the long term. The productivity of our meetings is up, too.[16]

In the Diocese of Davenport, Journey to Justice and the follow-up activities have therefore transformed individuals, clusters of parishes (deaneries), and the very structure of social action committee meetings.

Lessons of Journey to Justice

We can count the novel way of running church committee meetings described above as one of the most positive outcomes of Journey to Justice. Imagine proposing this change in your parish. A likely reaction: "We can't turn over one-third of our meeting to prayer and reflection; we've got work to do!" But Ebener insists that more work gets done when these retreat elements are adopted in committee meetings. I think he's on to something.

After reading this chapter you may be inspired to contact CCHD and schedule a Journey to Justice retreat in your parish. Great idea! But even if you do not, try what Dan Ebener learned from the Journey to Justice experience. Spend the first one-third of a social action committee meeting on faith formation. You might be surprised at how productive the next hour is.

A second lesson is simply to invite Jesus to dinner. Journey to Justice is the best model available for immersion experiences with the poor. But it is not the only way to have a dialogue with people living in poverty. Start with a conversation between parishioners and low-income people who defy the typical stereotypes. *Nothing* overcomes negative beliefs better than relationships. A face-to-face encounter with the poor allows parishioners to overcome prejudice and relate to others as neighbor. If you decide to organize an immersion experience, remember two essential elements: a formation component (scripture and Catholic social teaching) and the invitation of empowered people living in poverty (contact your diocesan CCHD director for suggestions). The empowered poor inspire hope not pity, partnership not paternalism. Follow the example of Journey to Justice; it is an Easter experience in a Good Friday world.

A final lesson concerns follow up. As I conducted background research for this chapter, I became convinced that the Journey to Justice retreat *by itself* will not fundamentally change individuals and parishes. Indeed, CCHD intends Journey to Justice to be a three-step process: planning, retreat, and follow up, although the last step appears to be weak in some places. What you have *not* read in this chapter are the stories of parishes that held the retreat and generated a lot of energy for social ministry, but allowed that energy to dissipate by expecting enthusiasm to translate to action by itself. According to the diocesan social action directors that I interviewed for background on Journey to Justice, the energy for social ministry dissipates within a year or two without a plan for follow up. One director noted sadly, "Two years later, you'd never know the retreat even happened."

But the focus of this book is on the success stories. You have learned how Journey to Justice successfully shaped social ministry in three locations. Why did these retreats succeed in drawing new leaders into lasting commitments to social ministry? Each of these Journey to Justice retreats fostered an experience of *conversion*, the "My Lord and my God!" experience. But in all of these cases, an organizer (Rita Waldref, Marjorie O'Sullivan, Dan Ebener) also called "Follow me!" to the retreatants, building momentum and interest through *invitation*. It is a hybrid experience of Christ that does not leave the fruits of *conversion* to chance. We will learn more about this dual experience of Christ drawing Catholics out of the middle pew in the next chapter, "Global Solidarity."

4

Global Solidarity and the Middle Pew

Like Journey to Justice, many short-term Catholic missionary programs utilize Christ's tool of *conversion* to engage new leaders in social ministry. Whereas Journey to Justice promotes face-to-face dialogue with people living in poverty in the United States, missionary programs take ordinary Catholics out of the middle pew and bring them into dialogue with the global poor. Mission, understood broadly, is proclaiming the gospel. One consequence of that mission is social action—the mission programs that you will encounter in this chapter. These one- to two-week global solidarity projects are sometimes called reverse missionary experiences because an important, perhaps primary, dimension of the short-term missionary project is the education and formation of the volunteer. In this chapter we examine how three such programs successfully engage middle-pew Catholics in the social mission of the church, drawing out the lessons they teach us about developing new social action leaders. As the following anecdote illustrates, there are special challenges to promoting global solidarity, such as the American tendency to swim against the current of global solidarity within Catholicism.

Who Is My Neighbor?

It never fails. I have been leading Catholic social-teaching workshops in the Archdiocese of New York for eight years. When we reach the topic of global solidarity, invariably a parishioner will ask: "Why are we concerned about the problems of other countries when we have so many problems in New York City? Shouldn't we deal with those issues first?"

Over the years, I have learned to be more patient with these folks. It is an understandable tribal reaction: to take care of one's own before responding to others. The problem is that this is not a Catholic view. When Jesus said, "Love…your neighbor as yourself" (Luke 10:27) and "Just as I have loved you, you also should love one another" (John 13:34–35), he did not add, "within these geopolitical boundaries." The words of Jesus in the parable of the good Samaritan do much to undermine such distinctions.

Today, I answer the question in two ways. First, I explain that our faith calls us to love our neighbors whether they live next door or across the globe. I invite parishioners to place themselves within Matthew 25 and imagine peering over the geopolitical fences we erect, at the wounded Christ who hungers for basic nutrition: *I was hungry and you gave me no food.* Second, I ask if, in an era of globalization, we can honestly say that the problems of New York City are not somehow connected to the problems of the rest of the world. Whether we like it or not, global issues affect domestic conditions, for example, HIV/AIDS in Africa (loss of potential markets for US goods), worker justice in China (loss of US manufacturing jobs), and the general health of the Mexican economy (immigration issues).

Reverse Missionaries

We belong to a global church with a global mission. Over the centuries Catholic missionaries have brought the faith to every nation on the globe. Today, a significant number of North American Catholics have taken on a new kind of missionary spirit, one that challenges the missionary as much as it brings hope to the poor. Many of today's Catholic missionaries are themselves evangelized by their missionary experience, working to improve the lives of neighbors in less developed nations. These Catholics have stood before Christ in a foreign land and cried out, "My Lord and my God!"

In most cases these missionaries claim that they receive far more than they give. The spirituality, awareness of other cultures, and leadership skills that they develop far outweigh the hard work and personal sacrifice of mission work. Many reflect later that they learned more from people in need than they taught. For this reason some experts on Catholic missiology have taken to calling these missionaries reverse missionaries.

Maria Nordone understands this term. Huddled in a stairwell in a building south of the World Trade Center on September 11, 2001, she realized that she wanted to make changes in her life. Nordone left a successful career on Wall Street and began a one-year sabbatical of "travel and adventure." A cousin from Atlanta invited Nordone to join her on a church mission trip to Nicaragua. Nordone fit the trip in between a Florida vacation and a kayaking trip in Mexico. The missionary group planned to build a chapel at an orphanage for children with disabilities. What Nordone saw at the Mustard Seed Communities orphanage surprised her:

> I expected to see miserable children when I went to Nicaragua, like on TV, when they want you to sponsor a child. At Mustard Seed the children have disabilities and have been abandoned. You expect to see these miserable crying children, but all you see are these happy, smiling, beautiful faces of kids who are just so happy to see us. They have nothing. They have no toys, they've got one set of clothes and they're on their back. They have no parents, but they are just so eager to love.[1]

Another time Nordone spoke of her experience:

> On my first day at the Mustard Seed home in Managua, I met a bright and beautiful five-year-old girl named Yelyi [pronounced jel-jee]. She and the other children were devouring a crate of toys that we brought down for them. While the other little girls grabbed the baby dolls and the boys grabbed the toy cars and trucks, I saw Yelyi pick up a new deck of playing cards. I was anxious to practice my Spanish, so I sat down beside her and taught

her a few simple card games, and we quickly became best friends. Over the course of the week, whenever I could take a break from the construction project, Yelyi and I would play cards.

On the day that we were leaving, Yelyi and I said a very teary goodbye. As I turned away to say goodbye to some of the other children, I saw Yelyi slip the deck of cards into my bag. I was shocked because this deck of cards was the only "toy" that Yelyi claimed as her own. I knelt down beside her and told her that the cards were for her to keep. She looked at me and said, "No, mama, they are for you to bring home with you...so you remember me."[2]

Nordone never forgot Yelyi. Indeed, she returned to the Mustard Seed orphanage several times and became Yelyi's godmother at baptism. Sixteen months after their first encounter, Nordone adopted Yelyi. Nordone now serves as executive director of Mustard Seed Communities USA, leading its US operations.

Art Sheridan is another Catholic whose life changed after becoming involved in global missions. He signed up for the construction corps of Partnership in Mission, the mission project of the Diocese of Joliet (Illinois) in Sucre, Bolivia, because "there's a point in your life that you realize that you've been blessed. And you want to share that."[3] In 1997 he joined the first construction group going to Bolivia, not without some trepidation. He recalls:

Our son had gone with some people to Appalachia, leading a week-long trip with high school kids. I said, "Art, what if I don't know what I'm going to do or I don't have the skills, what should I do?" And he said, "Dad, just stand with the people. Affirm them. Listen to them. Let them know that you are there *with* them, not trying to do something *for* them. About midway through the mission in Sucre I stood on this balcony overlooking the city, and I started crying. I realized that it was the wisdom of my son that gave me the ability to make the transition from trying to do things and rescue people, to just be and to listen.[4]

Sheridan spent two weeks in Bolivia, plastering houses, praying, and spending time with local people. He says that he was profoundly affected by the new relationships:

> I saw the poverty in a different way. I came back and realized that I could be part of changing the lifestyle of these people, so I joined the construction-corps board and tried to be more active. I also could no longer accept what I read in the paper as being the whole truth. I began to see that the marginalized and the poor don't have a voice. That's when my wife and I got involved in transitional housing and different activities with our Christian service commission at the parish.[5]

Sheridan went on the construction-corps trip with an attitude of trying to help the poor, to give back some of what God had given him. While he truly helped people by plastering their houses (thus preventing some insect-borne diseases), the transformation in his own life was even more profound. Sheridan recently left a career in the corporate world to become director of missions for the Diocese of Joliet.

Sheridan and Nordone were both peripheral to the social mission of the church before their experience of Christ in a developing country. They certainly were not opposed to social justice, but neither was it a priority in their lives. But someone they trusted recognized their potential and called "Follow me!" And when they met Jesus at the Mustard Seed orphanage in Nicaragua and among the poor of Sucre, Bolivia, they cried "My Lord and my God!" and began a commitment to social ministry.

The one-week mission trip is ideal for reverse missioners like Nordone and Sheridan: long enough to be immersed in the experience, away from the distractions of everyday life, but short enough to fit in with work and family life. How that week is structured is crucial. Good models of Catholic mission trips abound. The Catholic Network for Voluntary Service maintains a comprehensive website with information on many such programs. Here we focus on three mission trips, each of which offers a key lesson about engaging new leaders in Catholic social ministry. First, Mustard

Seed Communities demonstrates that time spent with Jesus in adoration and other prayer forms enhances the experience of Christ in
the poor. Second, the Diocese of Joliet's Partnership in Mission
teaches us that an emphasis on relationships and social analysis during the trip and concrete social action vehicles afterward promotes
greater conversion and development of new social justice leaders.
Finally, the Diocese of St. Cloud's partnerships with the Diocese of
Maracay, Venezuela, and the Diocese of Homa Bay, Kenya, show
that a focus on faith life in mission partnerships can draw leaders
who might not otherwise show interest in social ministries.

Tithing Prayer:
Mustard Seed Communities

Each mission trip differs in structure: how much time is devoted to
prayer; how much time is spent on projects like construction, child
care, medical treatment, and so on; and how much time is allotted
to reflecting on the ministry. Each mission trip involves an
encounter with Jesus, but few are as intentional about that experience as Mustard Seed Communities, an international network of
homes for children with disabilities who have been abandoned or
orphaned and a collection of economic development projects (a
bakery; a print shop; a pottery shop; a cyber-café; and fish, chicken,
and pepper farms). Fr. Gregory Ramkissoon, director of Mustard
Seed Communities and a priest of the Diocese of Kingston in
Jamaica, structures encounters with Christ throughout the mission
experience. He explains the children's role in the spiritual transformation of missioners:

> We all have to look at our rejected stones to become the
> cornerstones of our spiritual life. We have to make our-
> selves open to others—a totally disabled child, for
> example—who have nothing to offer us in our eyes, and
> we think that we have everything to offer them. The
> mission experience is to be naked in front of the children
> and in front of Christ.[6]

In addition to working with the children, Mustard Seed Communities requires that missionaries tithe 10 percent of the day in prayer. Eucharistic adoration, morning prayer, and evening prayer are the most popular ways that staff and volunteers meet the 2.4 hour per day prayer requirement. The disabled children themselves often lead the prayers, explains Fr. Ramkissoon, "because they are great repositories of prayer. Children who speak will, in their own way, sing hymns of praise, others will remain very quiet, others will say the rosary in their own way."[7]

Liturgical practices and popular devotions like the sacrament of reconciliation, the Stations of the Cross, and the Mass itself also provide the staff and volunteers opportunities to tithe 2.4 hours of daily prayer. The emphasis on prayer and encountering the poorest of the poor (disabled orphans in developing countries) keeps the focus on Jesus. As Fr. Ramkissoon explains:

> Jesus is the center because adoration is at the center of what we are doing. The second place we find Jesus is in our clients, so to speak, the children. Because we feel that Jesus is not only in the sacrament, in the bread of adoration, he is also with us in the most difficult circumstances of a child. Often, the child cannot walk, cannot talk. The only thing that child has to offer is to let Jesus shine through him or her. The third place we find Jesus is in the liturgical practices of the church.[8]

Mustard Seed provides an ideal reverse missionary experience. Certainly the children with Down syndrome, cerebral palsy, hydrocephalus, and other birth defects benefit from the love and attention provided by the volunteers, not to mention from the various construction projects. But the volunteers experience a transformative encounter with Christ, brought about by a synergy of prayer and social ministry. These moments of conversion spur many to make commitments to social ministry that would not otherwise occur.

Fr. Ramkissoon stresses that the real aim of the mission trips is the development of the volunteers, "to get them to become more aware of the presence of Christ in their ordinary lives, and do social justice programs back in their home parishes in a way that has a depth and an awareness to it."[9] He is the first to admit, however, that the trips are better at producing repeat volunteers than action for justice at home. He attributes this phenomenon to a lack of follow up with the energized returning volunteers:

> If they are not fed when they get back to Parish A or Parish B, the volunteers fall right back, six months after, into old ways of behavior. So we have had a lot of repeats. Some people come ten times. It tells me that they are not being fed in their parishes.[10]

For this reason Mustard Seed Communities has written *Work the Word*, published in 2005 by Paulist Press, a two-part (before and after the trip) formation process to shepherd volunteers to local action after their Mustard Seed experience.

A Short-Term Mission with a Long-Term Vision: Partnership in Mission

While Mustard Seed Communities excels at integrating the experience of Christ in the poor with the experience of Jesus in adoration and prayer, the Diocese of Joliet's Partnership in Mission serves as a model process of drawing volunteers into a commitment to social action ministries. The project began a decade ago, when the diocesan social action director, Tom Garlitz, aspired to develop a mission trip for Catholics that would also be "a laboratory experience for them, through service, to be formed for social justice."[11]

Garlitz teamed up with Dr. Enrique Vinrique, a physician of Bolivian origin, who had experienced mission trips with Protestants and wanted to develop a Catholic mission experience. Working with the Diocese of Sucre, Bolivia, they created a medical partnership assisted by Fr. Joachim Sanchez, a Sucre pastor, and a team of local surgeons. The local team in Bolivia now determines the medical needs of the poorest of the poor, and the Diocese of Joliet leadership looks at how Partnership in Mission can best meet those needs. In the early years of the program the medical missionaries discovered that God was calling them to additional ministries beyond the initial surgeries. Garlitz explains:

> In doing the surgeries we realized that, in a lot of instances, the cases that were presenting themselves had ties to sanitation, and that's when the construction mission was born, at first installing bathrooms in people's homes. In addition, they used to have to go down to the river… but now they can have potable water right at their house.

Garlitz and his partners found that many intestinal problems could be averted by public-health approaches. In addition, they discovered that a widespread heart ailment known as Chagga's Disease could be prevented by plastering the adobe brick of Bolivian homes. An insect that lives in adobe brick bites children as they sleep, causing Chagga's Disease. The illness causes an enlarged heart to develop twenty years later, preventing any work or physical activity. "It's much cheaper to plaster these homes than to insert a pacemaker in the patients, which is what we did in the early years of the mission," Garlitz explains.

Partnership in Mission has had a tremendous impact on public health in Sucre: 850 operations performed, a hospital and surgical center constructed, 864 homes plastered and/or provided with indoor plumbing. But it has had an equally impressive impact on the lives of the volunteers and the social action ministry of the Diocese of Joliet. Garlitz recalls that he and other architects of the program deliberately chose the comparatively slower path of developing relationships over accumulating even more impressive medical accomplishments:

> We are a short-term mission with a long-term vision. That means we're coming back. We don't just fly in and do something nice and then go home and feel good about it. We're there for the long haul. We build relationships, not just houses, and relationships take priority over the service. Unlike other groups, we don't do marathon surgery, we don't try to rack up the biggest sta-

tistics. So there is time built in to get to know the local doctors, to get to know the culture, to get out into the barrios and to see where the patients are coming from.[12]

Garlitz notes that in addition to the relationship-centered service, volunteers participate in a formation process prior to the trip to Sucre. Formation begins with an informational meeting, followed by two evening discussions and a weekend retreat. Participants learn about the spirituality of mission, Catholic social teaching, the culture of Bolivia, the crucial political issues facing Bolivians, and the logistics of the mission trip.

When volunteers return to Joliet, they attend a debriefing meeting where they are invited to join the diocesan public-policy network and consider other ways of taking action. Garlitz estimates that over half become involved in some aspect of the social action office's work. Only one-third of returning volunteers make a repeat trip, though many more wish to do so. The organizers encourage participants to put their energy back into ministries of the social action office and limit repeat participation.

Doug Casper is a volunteer who became deeply involved in Joliet's social action office after participating in a Partnership in Mission trip. A professional bricklayer, Casper joined the construction brigade in 1999. He had been involved with church social justice work in the 1970s but had been inactive for many years because "there were few opportunities to get involved."[13] He was invited to accompany the construction brigade because of his professional experience. Moved by the poverty that he saw in Bolivia, he signed up for the diocesan Peace and Justice Institute. Casper and his wife began to take teen mothers into their home during their pregnancies. He also became involved in the School of the America's protests at Ft. Benning, Georgia, eventually serving a ninety-day sentence for civil disobedience. He calls this experience amazing because of the tremendous support that he received from strangers across the nation. Casper now coordinates the Partnership in Mission construction brigades.

Dr. Vic Trinkus, another missionary who became more deeply involved in social ministry after his first Partnership in Mission experience, found his entire world view altered:

I lived in a secular world before the trip, and now I live in a spiritual world. The world now is about God. I got to see God working in the world and came to realize that it's not about me, it's about him. I fully believe that he did become man and die for our sins. If he did that, then I should work for him.[14]

Trinkus recalls that his conversion took place gradually during his first trip to Sucre, but intensified in a moment when he saw Christ himself:

I remember one specific experience when I walked up a street that goes to the Ricoletto, which is the original town of Sucre; it's about a thousand feet higher than the main city. I'd get up early around 5:30 and walk up this street. It's a steep climb, so it's a good workout. One time coming down I saw this man sitting in a doorway and if that wasn't him, then I've never seen him. I started to tear up at the thought of it, the eyes and the face. He just looked me square in the eyes and gave me this smile.[15]

My Lord and my God! Trinkus continues to maintain a full-time medical practice and now serves as medical director for Partnership in Mission, recently expanding the project to include trips to Colombia, Kenya, and the Philippines.

Many other participants in Partnership in Mission describe life-changing experiences through this short-term mission that led them to long-term commitments to social ministry. Some describe these experiences and follow-up actions as painful, but they all maintain that the experience made them better disciples. Dr. Lou Coda, who made a similar mission trip with the Catholic organization Mission Doctors, reflects on his experience of tumult after encountering the suffering of the poorest of the poor in developing nations:

Why subject myself to such an ugly part of life? Where is the pursuit of happiness in all of this? Why trust that below this boiling cauldron is a purifying fire? Because the only choice is to lay "asleep," anesthetized and slowly withering or to wake up and embrace a life that will not let me stay the same. I have heard the words a thousand times but not understood them, "It is by dying that we are born to eternal life." Stop thinking of where I want my life to go, what I want to be, but rather that it is enough to try and listen to the soft whispers of God calling us to trust and follow Him.[16]

In Coda's words one hears echoes of the JustFaith participants who discovered that they, too, were sleeping until awakened by God's call to act for justice. In addition, we hear again the theme of desirable discomfort, discomfort that spurs one to lifestyle change.

Rounding Up Unusual Suspects: Diocese of St. Cloud

When evaluating a social justice education event in the Archdiocese of New York, I always ask the question, "Did we simply draw 'the usual suspects'—Catholics already engaged in the social mission of the church—or did we expand our leadership base?" One church that has been very successful at engaging "unusual suspects" in social ministry through its Missions Office is the Diocese of St. Cloud. St. Cloud's approach is different from that of Mustard Seed Communities or Partnership in Mission in that the overt focus of the trips is not on social ministries but on relationship building. The diocese partners with the Diocese of Maracay, Venezuela, and the Diocese of Homa Bay, Kenya. The Maracay partnership has been in place for forty years, evolving from a one-way relationship of giving to an exchange of gifts and assets. The Homa Bay partnership began in 1999 through Catholic Relief Services' Harvest for Hope program.

In most Catholic dioceses, developing one global partnership is hard enough. But Bishop John Kinney has made mission activities a priority for the Diocese of St. Cloud, articulating his vision in a 1998 pastoral letter, *As I Have Done for You:*

We in the Diocese of St. Cloud have many ties to people in other parts of the world. Our population historically grew with immigrants arriving from Europe. In more recent decades, the population of Central Minnesota has grown and diversified with persons coming from less developed nations. These newer immigrants remind us of our ties to people all over the world. They remind us that we are members of one human family and that we share in the responsibility to help build one global community where the terms "First World" and "Third World" are obsolete.[17]

The diocesan partnerships focus on the church life of each diocese and the everyday lives of parishioners. Much of the sharing begins in the liturgical life of the church, cultural celebrations, and work and family life. Delegations from each diocese travel to the other annually as part of the exchange.

Fr. Bill Vos, missions director for the diocese, explains that the objective of the St. Cloud diocesan delegations is to enter into the lives of Catholics in Maracay and Homa Bay in an experiential way, two by two, living with families. He reports, "Invariably, the delegates say that it was a life-changing experience, because the methodology that we're using is to live as closely as possible to the people in their actual, real-life situations."[18] The partnerships also include annual visits from delegations of the diocesan partners to St. Cloud, so that more Catholics in the diocese may benefit from the exchange between the peoples and the visitors may learn about the lives of US Catholics.

The lack of a clear social ministry focus might appear to mitigate against awareness of social justice issues. But this view neglects to take into account the power of relationships to introduce social issues into the exchange. Fr. Vos elaborates on the "life-changing" experiences that he observes:

> The initial impact of going to Homa Bay or Maracay occurs when they observe the lifestyle of the people with whom they live. It's really very dramatic. The whole question of consumerism comes up. They realize how little others have to survive on, and yet the quality of life in these communities supersedes their own in many

ways. There are basic values of interdependence and sharing and the sense of community. When people sit and exchange views on these topics, it grounds them. They see what it means for them to have such a large chunk of the world's resources and the inequity of it all.[19]

Shirley Anderson is representative of many St. Cloud mission delegates. She articulates her experience as a delegate to Maracay:

Our visit to Venezuela has made me more aware that all people are brothers and sisters in Christ. Many years ago, my husband and I lived in Ada, Minnesota, where Mexican migrants worked in the sugar beet fields. Several times, families hoed sugar beets in the fields that joined our yard. The migrant workers would put down blankets at the edge of the field for the children to sit on while their parents worked. It makes me very sad and ashamed that I ignored these dear people. I never offered them a drink of cold water. I didn't even invite them to leave their children in the shade of our yard. I hope that I will never more ignore my fellow man. I want to extend the courtesy and kindness shown to us by the people of Venezuela.[20]

Anderson returned from her participation in the delegation to Maracay with an increased solidarity with the people of Maracay and with all people. Her new passion for mission led her to work with her parish to set up a formal partnership between St. Anne's Parish in Brandon, Minnesota, and Parroquia Inmaculada Concepción in Barbacoas, Venezuela.

The experience of solidarity felt by those who host delegations from a partner diocese or travel to the partner diocese often leads to a solid look at their previous attitudes toward other groups; prejudices they may not have questionned are overcome in interactions with the "other." Forty years of partnership with the Diocese of Maracay and six years of connecting with the Diocese of Homa Bay have indeed affected class-based and ethnicity-based prejudices, but the partnerships have also fostered the conviction among delegates and others that legislative advocacy is necessary to confront the social problems faced by Catholics worldwide. Fr. Vos explains:

> When these people come back, they try to dig into how they can use their experience for a significant change. They realize that taking up a collection is fine, there's a place for that, but the impact and the significance of change is so much greater if they can take action on the political level. A lot of our delegates have also become more active locally. It's the people who have gone to Kenya and to Venezuela who are acting to save the safety net for women, children, and the homeless here.[21]

Fr. Vos notes that a large number of returning delegates have become key leaders in parish social justice committees. Many of the leaders involved in the partnership are involved in debt-relief efforts for the poorest indebted nations and advocate for increased funding for global HIV/AIDS prevention and treatment. The diocesan Homa Bay Partnership Committee also includes a subcommittee on legislative advocacy that promotes activity on Catholic Relief Services' legislative action alerts. The initial focus on nonpolitical aspects of mission does not seem to discourage eventual political advocacy, an outcome Fr. Vos credits to a diocesan strategy of continued engagement through legislative networks, speaking tours, parish partnerships, and solidarity committees.

Conversion and Mission Trips: Four Lessons

Each of these models offers a set of lessons for engaging new leaders in the social mission of the church. First, Mustard Seed Communities teaches us that we must do more than reveal Christ in the poor. We must also give missioners time to encounter Jesus through eucharistic adoration and other prayer forms. Mustard Seed demonstrates that one experience of Christ reinforces the other.

Second, we learn from Partnership in Mission that we must harness the passion that volunteers return with by providing training opportunities and concrete vehicles for action. The relationships so carefully cultivated in Bolivia are honored by the continued action of returning delegates and missioners. As in Journey to Justice retreats, we must follow mission trips with further opportunities for leadership development in social action lest the energy dissipate.

Third, we need to recognize from the St. Cloud experience that some "unusual suspects" will be drawn into mission work if we center the experience solely around relationship building in the beginning. We may start with a focus diverted from social ministry, but we must have confidence that, with encouragement, missioners will ultimately become concerned with social action. Our leadership base will become all the more diverse as a result.

Finally, we should note that the leaders of many programs offering mission trips report a higher percentage of men involved than women. Perhaps it is the adventure, perhaps it is the construction projects, perhaps mission trips serve as a clear way to bring meaning into the lives of these men. In any case, the interest of men in mission work is a phenomenon often unseen in social ministry, where females typically far outnumber males. A parish interested in drawing more men into social ministry would do well to consider developing a short-term mission trip.

Like JustFaith and Journey to Justice, these three short-term mission trips demonstrate the possibilities of conversion as a means of drawing new adult leaders into social ministry. But what about youth? Aren't they the future of the church? No, youth are part of the *present* of the church, and many have indeed become young prophets of justice through an experience of conversion. Chapter 5 focuses on conversion experiences among adolescent Catholics.

5

❖

Young Prophets of Justice

The three previous chapters focus on applying Christ's tool of conversion with groups of Catholic adults. This chapter examines the application of conversion to ministry with Catholic youth and young adults from the early teens through college age. In this chapter we explore successful service-learning programs[1] that introduce young people to Catholic social ministry through time-limited "My Lord and my God!" experiences. These programs bring adolescents face to face with the Christ of Matthew 25 in developmentally appropriate ways. We examine these ministries and the reasons for their success, drawing out lessons about engaging young middle-pew Catholics in the social mission of the church. We begin with a failure that has much to teach us.

A Service Project That Missed the Point

The Worst Service Project Ever

I meant well; I really did.

When I accepted the position as parish youth minister for a large parish in Springfield, Missouri, I inherited a three-year confirmation program for teens composed of numerous requirements and prerequisites, including ten hours of community service. Most of the youth hated the service hours they were asked to perform, viewing them either as punishment or as a kind of purgation experience (complete your hours and a proportional volume of sins would be forgiven). Rarely did parish youth imagine service as part of their baptismal call. At best, they saw community service as just one more hoop to jump through before "graduating" with the sacrament of confirmation.

When I first discussed the service project with the volunteer coordinator of a local shelter, it seemed like a good idea. He invited the youth of our parish to clean up the grounds of the homeless shelter before the city's annual Memorial Day parade. It was an image-enhancement effort on the part of the shelter. In the past, parade-goers had complained of trash in the street, blaming it on the homeless. The shelter wanted to remove any question of its association with loose trash in the street and the implication (believed by many) that it dealt in human trash.

Twenty parish youth appeared at 9:00 a.m. for roll call and orientation. We quickly learned that cleaning up the grounds meant combing what appeared to be an endless supply of cigarette butts out of the shelter's large front lawn. We set to work with leaf rakes and gloves, raking together giant piles of butts and then bagging them.

A passerby asked me what the teens were doing. I explained that the kids were cleaning up the grounds before the parade. She exclaimed, "They sure are giving out light sentences these days." I replied indignantly, "They're a church group, ma'am." She apologized, and we continued working. I later thought the woman was the one who had it right. It looked like punishment; it felt like punishment; it smelled like punishment.

The day grew hot and muggy. We kept on. It seemed that the cigarette butts were as numerous as the grains of sand on the shore or the stars in the sky. Perhaps God missed a good metaphor in his promises to Abraham: "Your descendants will be as numerous as the cigarette butts on the lawn of the shelter." We grew sweaty and cranky. One girl asked, "How come these people can't feed their kids, but they have money for cigarettes?" Good question. We began a bitter social-analysis session to pass the time.

I realize now that I didn't prepare the parish youth and as a result they served merely as unpaid trash collectors for the shelter. There was no way they were going to see Christ in a the experience. I had failed them as a formation director. I had not set up any opportunities to meet the homeless families. I offered no reflection opportunities before or after the service experience about the causes and effects of homelessness.[2] Nor had I prepared them for the day with scripture readings or explorations of Catholic social teaching. We didn't even pray. I had offered the youth of the parish little more than an opportunity to reinforce stereotypes about the poor.

Serving Christ with Head, Heart, and Hands

The fields of youth ministry and community service have evolved quite a bit since my days on the front lines. During the past decade major foundations and researchers have studied secular and religious service and service-learning programs to uncover best practices and to discern the effects of service on youth and young adults. Teachers and youth ministers have reflected on their experiences and redesigned programs to reflect the trial-and-error wisdom of three decades of ministry. Most important, many bishops, Catholic college presidents, principals, pastors, teachers, and youth ministers have realized that facilitating encounters with Jesus Christ and helping young people understand those encounters is far more important than the number of hours worked. This chapter draws from the wisdom of these leaders in Christian service and examines the ingredients for success in bringing young people into encounters with Christ and commitments to social ministry.

Robert McCarty, director of the National Federation for Catholic Youth Ministry, views the aim of youth and young-adult service to be an encounter with Jesus. Good service "is meeting up with God's predilection for the poor," he explains. It is an evangelizing moment, when youth "meet God in the face."[3] McCarty's description recalls the experiences of adult conversion described earlier. Through proper preparation for service, relational experiences with poor and vulnerable people, and thoughtful processing of those experiences, youth also experience the Christ of Matthew 25 among the hungry, the aged, and the persons with handicaps whom they serve. Like Thomas, they too cry out "My Lord and my God!" as they are drawn into a new spirituality of social mission.

Indeed, it is the spirituality of service, or *diakonia*, that distinguishes Christian efforts from the many secular options in the world of volunteerism. Pamela Reidy, a veteran of Catholic school-based service-learning programs, argues that Christians must, from the start, draw from their own spirituality.

> The inherent difference between service learning in Catholic educational settings and the service experiences mandated by the courts, assigned by the public school, or offered by secular organizations is in the expressed motive and intended outcome. The sole purpose of Christian ministry is to bring about the reign of God, and the intended outcome is complete and unconditional love.[4]

Reidy believes that in baptism we accept the call to service. Therefore all of our efforts to serve God by serving the poor and vulnerable flow from that sacrament. No other rationale (or arm twisting) need be applied. Simply put, if we are serious about being Christians, we have to be serious about serving the "least of these."

Noting that the call to live out baptismal commitments should be delivered in developmentally appropriate ways, Reidy suggests different approaches to service with both younger and older adolescents. Developmentally, young adolescents, aged eleven to fifteen, need to develop relationships with a variety of people and acquire a sense of belonging to a peer group. According to the American Academy of Child and Adolescent Psychiatry (and confirmed by millions of parents), young adolescents are relentlessly focused on themselves, alternating between high expectations and poor self-esteem. They demonstrate an improved ability to express themselves and are physically and intellectually capable of new kinds of work. They are mostly interested in the present moment, with limited thoughts of the future. They are beginning to develop ideals and role models even as they distance themselves from parents.[5] They often have more free time than older teens because they do not yet hold jobs or have a driver's license.[6] Reidy explains:

> Desperately desiring to belong and setting aside child-like behaviors, teenagers search for heroes, significant adults, and a group membership that feels safe. With

these securities, they can become comfortable asking life's meaningful questions: Who am I? Who am I becoming? What am I? What do I want to be? Service-learning allows these fragile identity-seekers to experience independence and individual choices that reinforce a developing sense of autonomy.[7]

The differences in cognitive abilities suggest an architecture of service opportunities for early and middle adolescents. Reidy recommends single-event service opportunities for younger adolescents. Experiencing a variety of these "one shot" experiences helps them identify interests and skills in the context of a supportive environment.

Older adolescents (aged sixteen to twenty-two[8]), on the other hand, are capable of more extended commitments. The American Academy of Child and Adolescent Psychiatry describes them as possessing a firmer and more cohesive sense of identity. They show clear concern for others, demonstrate the ability to examine inner experiences and apply moral reasoning, and indicate a reawakened interest in cultural and social traditions, shelved as patently uncool in early adolescence.[9] The increased cognitive and emotional capacities provide new opportunities for reflection on scripture and church teaching that do not exist for younger adolescents. As Reidy writes:

> Older adolescents approach moral matters with a greater degree of reasoning, allowing them to bring greater awareness to their service experience. The ability to critique social values and recognize moral imperatives changes the service experience from "doing good to feel good" to a response of moral necessity. Universal principles can be more easily considered, as the young adult will now internalize a moral value system. Justice and love as components of service now go beyond "what I am supposed to do" as the teenager can comprehend the interrelationship of these essential elements. For this reason, it is essential to fortify them with Catholic social teaching.[10]

The social doctrine of the church provides an interpretive lens for youth and young adults who take part in activities that help them see beyond acts of charity to works of justice.

Reidy suggests that teachers, youth ministers, campus ministers, and professors present the church's social teaching to older adolescents, giving special attention to the pope's annual World Youth Day messages, which often contain social lessons.[11] For example, in 1996, in preparation for the Twelfth World Youth Day, Pope John Paul II presented this message to the youth of the world:

> *Jesus is living next to you*, in the brothers and sisters with whom you share your daily existence. His visage is that of the *poorest*, of the marginalized who, not infrequently, are victims of an unjust model of development, in which profit is given first place and the human being is made a means rather than an end.[12]

Imagine, for a moment, a group of teens just completing service at a soup kitchen. If it is a typical group, many of the teens are disturbed by some aspect of what they have seen and heard. Most have questions about the guests. A few are so moved that they wish to take a dramatic step in response. A message from the pope expressly addressed to youth serving people living in poverty is one of the most pastoral responses youth ministers, teachers, and campus ministers can provide.

Young Catholics need Catholic social teaching, but they need that teaching offered with all its nuances. Theological reflection on scripture and Catholic social teaching is therefore one of the main ingredients for success in adolescent service and service-learning programs. This interpretive lens appeals to the *head* (and older adolescents' developing faculties of moral reason). But Bob McCarty, director of the National Federation for Catholic Youth Ministry, explains that while the best service-learning programs include reflection on Catholic social teaching (head), they also draw attention to the teachings of Jesus on compassion, Matthew 25 in particular (heart). And effective training on the specifics of how to do service in the expected milieu prepares young people for action (hands).

For example, young people need to learn what to call those who eat at the soup kitchen (good: guests; bad: the less fortunate; worse: bums). They need to know how to respond if a guest asks for a second helping. They need suggestions and even practice to learn to speak appropriately to the guests.[13] McCarty insists that if proper attention is paid to preparing the head, heart, and hands, youth and young adults will be well equipped for the experience of service and its effects will be long lasting.

A second requirement for effective Christian service is a relational structure. Young people must have the opportunity to meet Jesus if the faculties of the heart are to be awakened. They won't meet Jesus in a cigarette butt when they are working cleanup, or in a nail or screw if they are working on a construction project. That is why the best service organizations find creative ways for *relational* aspects of service projects to emerge. For example, Habitat for Humanity requires the families who will own the home to work alongside the Habitat volunteers for a specified number of hours. The volunteers and the needy thus become acquainted.[14]

Fr. Bill Lies, CSC, director of the University of Notre Dame's Center for Social Concerns, likes to underscore the importance of the face-to-face encounter with people living in poverty by telling the story of a recent Notre Dame faculty seminar with liberation theologian Gustavo Gutiérrez. Lies recalls that during the seminar a faculty member described a disappointing encounter with a freshman:

> A young man in her class said, "This is great, all of this talk about the poor. I'd do something about it, but the thing is, I don't really care." She was absolutely flabbergasted. She asked Gutiérrez, "What do you do with that?" He replied, "We can talk about the poor, we can teach about the poor, we can read about the poor, but until we meet them, until we come face to face with them, and our lives interplay with their lives, our students are not going to 'get it.'"[15]

Fr. Lies estimates that the Notre Dame's undergraduate college offers 120 community-based learning courses and seminars throughout the curriculum. For Fr. Lies, the encounter with people in need is critical, but so is the conversation with Catholic social teaching and the student's own academic discipline. A chemistry course taught by Professor Dennis Jacobs provides a good example. Wanting to design a course that would "touch the world," Professor Jacobs developed the "Lead Course," in which students not only learn about lead but also test for its presence in older homes in poor South Bend neighborhoods. He conducts the course in partnership with South Bend's Memorial Hospital and the county Get the Lead Out task force. The course shows students how chemistry interacts with issues of social importance even as they are challenged by Catholic social teaching to apply the church's social doctrine to their work.

Service Learning Works

If you want to learn about the profound changes many students experience through service-learning programs, anecdotal evidence abounds. To the breathless accounts of youth, young adults, parish youth ministers, teachers, and campus ministers, we can now add the results of empirical research by the Higher Education Research Institute (HERI) at the University of California at Los Angeles. The HERI research is regarded as the definitive study of service and service learning among those who work with service-learning and community-service programs, although it deals almost entirely with secular aspects of service and service learning. The study focused on the college student cohort within the older adolescent group, but most service-learning experts believe that the results would also hold true for sixteen- to eighteen-year-old high school students. Because of their relative lack of emotional and cognitive maturity, it would be difficult to infer similar results for early adolescents.

In this long-term study of 22,236 undergraduate college students attending American colleges and universities, HERI studied a group divided as follows: 30 percent participated in course-based service learning, 46 percent participated in service alone, and 24 percent did not participate in any kind of service in college.[16] Among those participating in service-learning programs, the researchers found positive effects on grades, increases in values such as "commitment to activism" and "promoting racial understanding," growth in interpersonal skills, and increases in the percentages of students who chose a service career or planned to participate in service after college. The findings were consistent with previous, smaller studies. Three of the researchers' conclusions stand out:

- When discussion is part of the service or service-learning process, the positive outcomes described above are more pronounced. Typically, service-learning courses generate more discussion than service experiences without a classroom component.
- The greatest factor contributing to the success of service-learning experiences is how interested students are in the topic. The second most important factor is "whether the professor encourages class discussion."
- Service-learning works in part because "it facilitates four types of outcomes: an increased sense of personal efficacy, an increased awareness of the world, and increased awareness of one's personal values, and increased engagement in the classroom experience."[17]

The HERI study supports most of Reidy's conclusions, despite its secular limitations. Other studies note that K-12 service-learning programs increase participants' academic achievement,[18] and that participation in college service-learning experiences increases both career choices in service fields and increased civic activities.[19] Some Catholic universities have commissioned internal studies that affirm many of the results of the HERI study and measure additional effects of service learning, such as changes in student attitudes toward people living in poverty.[20] A future HERI study, to be completed in 2006, will add some measures of religiosity and also measure civic engagement ten years after the service experience.

What remains to be formally studied on a wide scale is the relative effectiveness of approaches to religious instruction that utilize scripture and church teaching. For now, we simply have to trust the emerging consensus among those who have been perfecting their approaches to service over the past three decades of ministry: when head, heart, and hands are fully engaged, young disciples respond with a passion that makes adult Catholics proud and even a bit envious. Each youth minister, teacher, or campus minister who utilizes a model akin to McCarty's "head-heart-hands" can name "gazillions" (as one interviewee put it) of graduates whose lives were changed by the encounter with Christ in the poor. They point to former students who now lead chapters of Habitat for Humanity, serve immigrants seeking legal services, or live out their public service in local police or fire departments. Administrators at the University of Notre Dame frequently note the fact that 10 percent of Notre Dame graduates serve a year or more after graduation in programs such as the Jesuit Volunteer Corps and Holy Cross Associates.[21] These young adults are the potential next generation of top leadership in parish social ministry, so church leaders take heed!

Forming Prophets of Justice

Adolescents are drawn to service for both laudable (to live their ideals, to respond to those in need) and less laudable ("my parents are making me get confirmed," "my girlfriend was going on the trip") reasons. With the right guidance they flourish, and many are forever changed by the encounter with Christ in the poor. But do adolescents understand the difference between charity and justice? Can they do social action as well as direct service? These "two feet" of Christian service are often illustrated as side-by-side footprints, each necessary to move toward the kingdom of God, each essential to maintain balance. Simply put, direct service responds to immediate human suffering; social change removes the causes of the suffering. Gayle Zambito, director of youth ministry for Holy Family parish in Orlando, Florida, integrates the "two feet" into her CARE model (Catechesis-Action-Respect-Engagement). She encourages students to look at the justice dimensions of issues that they encounter during their service work, become involved in civil society through participation in student government and Orlando City Council commissions, and attend social justice events for youth like Peace Jam.

Left to their own devices, high school students tend to stick to direct service. But when a youth minister, teacher, or campus minister guides them in asking the right questions about the service experience, they can become prophets of justice. Pat Sprankle, youth ministry director for St. Louis Parish in Clarksville, Maryland, explains:

> In the Old and New Testaments, prophets spoke out because they felt called by God to speak out about justice issues. Micah 6:8 says, "To act justly, love tenderly, and walk humbly with your God, this is the most important thing." Amos also believed that the pyramid of the rich should be toppled so that the poor could have more power.
>
> Prophets back then were people who heard the word of God and acted upon it even if it meant standing alone. After conversations about the prophetic tradition, we ask the youth, "How can you be a prophet of justice, not only doing direct service, but also taking a look at some of the structures that cause injustice and doing something?"[22]

Every month Sprankle takes youth from his parish, located in one of the most affluent communities in the nation, to serve lunch to homeless people in Baltimore. The youth prepare five hundred lunches on site and then break to talk with staff about the causes of homelessness. They also discuss how they might converse with homeless people when lunch is served and learn about agencies that work with the homeless in Baltimore. Ultimately, many attend the state Catholic advocacy day sponsored by the Maryland Catholic Conference, encouraging legislators to respect human life in formulating legislation regarding abortion and poverty.

The jump from direct service to social action is sometimes difficult for older adolescents because many perceive politics as ethically tainted and service as morally pure. Dr. Kathleen Maas Weigert, director of Georgetown University's Center for Social Justice Research, Teaching, and Service, helps students take a more positive view of the public arena by ensuring that they engage in social analysis, like Sprankle's youth group, but she also stresses to students that the public arena is what they make of it:

The way we can help them move from a notion that service is a one-way street is to help them understand the issues in which that service is embedded. Example: You feed hungry people. You take that service and say: "Let's think about why it is that some people have this need at this moment in time in our society. What's happened to the economy? Where are jobs that allow people to live full human lives? Where is housing that allows them to live in decent shelter? Where are the schools that will allow them to have the right kind of education?"

What I try to help them understand is that it is a good thing to be involved, to be aware of who their congressperson is, who their local, state, national representatives are. And to help them understand the ease with which it is possible to contact legislators and make their opinions known. We try to help them understand that the public arena is one in which decisions are being made and politics is the vehicle for a lot of those decisions. Contacting elected officials is essential.[23]

Weigert wisely works to remove the stereotypes students have about politics, describing its core functions and explaining that political decisions can be made with or without their input. It is up to the students themselves whether they want to influence those decisions.

Megan Shepherd, assistant director of campus ministry for Ignatius College Prep in Chicago, Illinois, applied similar principles to an Appalachian work camp for high school students during her years as a parish youth minister. The parish had a longstanding relationship with the Appalachian Service Project (ASP) before Shepherd arrived, but student formation was not a priority. "What was really going on was, 'Let's get together, okay, does everyone know when the buses are leaving? Did we sell enough candy bars?'" she explains. Shepherd developed a year-long process for the ASP, with students applying in October to attend during the following summer. Five formation meetings helped students build community and explore the issues facing people living in Appalachia through the lens of Catholic social teaching. Youth who had made the trip previously shared stories, pictures, and in some cases, video, to help newcomers prepare. The ASP provided reflection experiences during the trip. Upon return, Shepherd conducted an exit interview with each youth. "I asked, 'Okay, what are you going to do now that you are back?'" She recalls. "In a lot of cases those students become my leaders for the next year."[24]

Shepherd also worked with the ASP to ensure that the youth considered social action approaches to the justice issues that they encountered. A group of Appalachian teens who had, through lobbying efforts, forced a mining company to build a fresh water pipeline to their town spoke to Shepherd's group about their work. Like Sprankle, Shepherd sees a dramatic increase in youth commitment to service—and to a lesser extent, to justice—among those who complete experiences like the ASP.

Sr. Linda Campbell, an academic advisor and coordinator at St. Mary's High School in Phoenix, Arizona, also makes reflection a priority in promoting consideration of justice issues. "It's easier to talk about the justice piece when they are in a large group," she maintains. "Students who do service on their own don't generally make those connections."[25] In short, journals and class assignments have their place, but there is nothing like peer-to-peer interaction led by a caring and knowledgeable adult.

Sean Lansing, program coordinator for Young Neighbors in Action in Milwaukee, Wisconsin, is another youth minister helping students make social justice connections. He utilizes the four-step pastoral circle first developed by Peter Henriot and Joe Holland: experience, social analysis, theological reflection, and action.[26] The key, Lansing argues, is social analysis. "Once they start asking questions, then they begin making connections." Through innovative, game-like exercises he encourages youth to understand the interplay between individual choices and structural causes of injustice. Lansing uses an activity called "the justice web" with high school students who attend the Young Neighbors in Action service weeks. The students take an issue that confronts them in service, like hunger, and begin to brainstorm causes of hunger. They each take the role of a particular cause and make connections among the causes by tossing a ball of yarn from one cause to the next. The result is a striking visual: a web of interrelated causes.[27]

College students tend to be capable of more abstract thinking and may not require a device like the justice web to help them do social analysis. The group discussions, however, are noted by Sr. Campbell and nearly all researchers on service learning as critical to a positive experience for these older adolescents. The adults who accompany college students on this journey take on a critical role.

Pam Rector, director for the Center for Service and Action at Loyola Marymount University in Los Angeles, always looks for opportunities to introduce legislative advocacy to students. For example, many of her students volunteer at a California juvenile detention facility. When state Assembly leaders introduced legislation to send juveniles to adult facilities, she raised the awareness of the student volunteers to the negative implications of the legislation. The students responded with telephone calls and letters to their home legislators. Rector believes that connecting service to action for justice is the key to developing "faithful citizenship."[28] She explains, "When students get into the habit of legislative advocacy, it's a skill that will continue on. If we get them to register, if we get them to vote, if we get them to write letters and make phone calls, we teach them what it means to be a Christian in this society."[29]

The Two Faces of Jesus:
Lessons for Parish Leaders

The aim of these leaders is simple: to form young prophets for justice. The complexity of formation is the difficult part; it is a ministry in which the adults who accompany young people take on particular importance. Adult mentors help young people recognize Christ in the people they serve and connect the needs of those people to social justice issues. Pat Sprankle articulates his own pedagogy in working with suburban Maryland youth at another Appalachian work camp:

> One of the questions we ask each night at the Appalachian workcamp is, "How did you see Jesus today? Where did you experience Christ's presence?" We have to ask that when we do service, because if we don't, we've missed

what it's all about. We see the face of Jesus in the poor.
That question gets one or two responses at the beginning of the week, but by the end of the week, we can't
stop them from talking, because they're now more aware
of how Jesus has impacted their experience.[30]

The recognition of Christ comes slowly for these young people,
and only in the company of a trusted mentor, but picks up speed in
the presence of peers. The key seems to be asking the right question (How did you see Jesus today?) in a climate of trust.

Jesus stands at both sides of the young person involved in
Christian service and social action. He is the person in need, the
Christ of Matthew 25. But Jesus also stands next young people calling
"Follow me!" He is the capable youth minister, the wise teacher or
professor, or the committed campus minister who uses Christ's tool of
invitation. Megan Shepherd articulates this aspect of the ministry:

Jesus is very present in awakening young hearts and
minds to serve. The disciples didn't get it right away. It
took time for them to grasp what Jesus was trying to do
in our world: proclaiming liberty, forgiving sins, and
bringing grace and reconciliation.

I believe that's what my ministry with young people
does. Jesus is the inspiration for it. He is alongside me
and helps give me the words when I need them. He
offers the grace that lights a spark in kids' eyes when they
really understand that you can bring as much food to a
family as you can carry, but something has to be done
about why they are not getting food on their own.[31]

In some ways, Shepherd suggests, the adult leader takes on the role
of Christ on the road to Emmaus (Luke 24:13–35), explaining the
scriptures to the confused and frightened disciples. We who are
responsible for the formation of young prophets would do well to
recognize this second critical role of Christ in engaging young
Catholics in the social mission of the church.

How should you begin to apply these lessons to your parish?
First, look at what already exists. Do the youth ministries in your

parish give young people an opportunity to meet Christ face to face in the poor and vulnerable? Does the service encouraged or required of youth include sessions with trusted adults that develop the faculties of head, heart, and hands? Does this reflection help adolescents make social justice connections and encourage social action as well as direct service?

Jesus loved the little children. But he didn't give up on them when they became adolescents. Neither should you and your parish overlook this critical period in the development of Catholics. Adolescents can be key leaders in social ministry. Whether they will maintain that commitment in parishes through their early and middle adulthood depends upon you.

PART III

Empowerment:
"Feed My Sheep"

6

Broad-Based Community Organizing

Jesus draws Catholics out of the middle pew through invitation and conversion, but he also calls us out through *empowerment.* Empowerment, the third of Jesus' three tools for engaging the middle pew, is the focus of Chapters 6 and 7. "Feed my sheep" (John 21:17) is the principle underlying empowerment. With empowerment, low-income Catholics identify with Christ and his suffering, seeing *themselves* on the cross yet resolving to live as resurrection people. They assume leadership in broad-based community organizations and worker justice groups, fed by a church that helps them develop both individual skills in public life and powerful mediating institutions.

In this chapter we look at broad-based community organizing, plumbing this application of Jesus' tool of empowerment for lessons to help us engage low-income Catholics in social ministry. Broad-based organizing networks like the Industrial Areas Foundation (IAF) develop organizations of organizations. They bring together mediating institutions such as religious congregations, civic associations, immigrant societies, and labor unions that act as a buffer between massive institutions in our society and the individual. We examine specific examples of broad-based organizing projects with a view to discerning how empowerment can help us to develop low-income leadership for Catholic social ministry. We begin with a telling anecdote from a Protestant clergyman.

"Feed My Sheep"

In *Blue Collar Ministry* church-development consultant Tex Sample tells the story of a fateful ride through the residential subdivisions of a small city. Sample, two mainline Protestant pastors, and a denominational executive formed the advance guard of a new congregation. The scouting trip was part of an effort to locate the new church at a location convenient to potential members. The trip would prove fateful to Sample's own development as well as the congregation's.

Seeing pickup trucks with gun racks and motorcycles parked in front yards in one neighborhood, a pastor remarked, "Well, I don't think we'll find many of our church members here....They just don't seem to be comfortable in our churches. Somehow we just don't seem to attract them."[1] In his book Sample examines working-class life in the United States and the church's ambiguous response to blue-collar subcultures.

Reading Sample's reflections, it occurred to me how frequently middle- and upper-middle-class Catholic social ministry leaders write off low-income parishioners. "Those people are just working so hard to get by. They're not interested in social justice. We tried. We invited them to meetings, but they don't come."

In many Catholic parishes a wealthier white congregation dominates parish leadership, but such homogenous leadership can obscure the existence of a second congregation within the first, comprising first- and second-generation immigrants of more modest means. These newcomers often worship at a separate Mass offered in their native language. Sometimes parish membership encompasses several economic classes, but the social justice committee may attract only those from the upper level of income.

The wealthier parishioners may well try to diversify the group. They invite. They place notices in the bulletin. They may even call "Follow me!" in their own way. But they ultimately fail to engage a significant pool of low-income parishioners. Like Bertha from Chapter 1, they place responsibility for the small numbers on the other parishioners, not on their own ineffective recruiting methods. The same goes for well-meaning church staff in predominantly working-class and poor parishes. They think that those closer to poverty should be more interested in social justice ministries than middle-class Catholics and express bafflement when their efforts yield little fruit.

The truth is that all Catholics are called to social ministry, but Christ draws people through varied means. A wealthy doctor might cry out "My Lord and my God!" on a Bolivian hillside, but low-income parishioners will be drawn into social ministry in a different way. It begins with *their* condition. Many working-class and poor Catholics find themselves nailed to a cross of social injustice. Their communities are wounded, sometimes pronounced dead by outside commentators, yet many do resolve to live as resurrection people, leading organizations like South Bronx Churches (SBC) and Upper Manhattan Together (UMT), broad-based community organizations in New York City affiliated with the IAF. These Catholics are intimately familiar with the wounded Christ of Matthew 25, but they also know the risen Christ, who triumphs over sin and death.

My experience is that a church willing to listen can engage low-income Catholics in social ministry simply by following Jesus' advice to Peter: "Feed my sheep." In John 21, Christ appears to the disciples for the third time after his resurrection, sharing breakfast with them around a charcoal fire. The evangelist writes:

> When they had finished breakfast, Jesus said to Simon Peter, "Simon son of John, do you love me more than these?" He said to him, "Yes, Lord; you know that I love you." Jesus said to him, "Feed my lambs." A second time he said to him, "Simon son of John, do you love me?" He said to him, "Yes, Lord; you know that I love you." Jesus said to him, "Tend my sheep."
>
> He said to him the third time, "Simon son of John, do you love me?" Peter felt hurt because he said to him the third time, "Do you love me?" And he said to him, "Lord, you know everything; you know that I love you." Jesus said to him, "Feed my sheep." (John 21:15–17)

When we read this passage today, we hear not only Jesus' instruction to "Simon son of John," but also Christ's command to the church itself. The message is clear: if we love Jesus, we must tend his flock.

Those concerned with promoting the church's social mission would do well to first look to the perceived needs, or self-interests, of this flock. If we seek to engage low-income Catholics in social ministry, we must first look at how injustice affects *them*. We must find out what makes them angry, what gets under their skin, what would change if they possessed the power to act effectively. Good social ministry with low-income Catholics doesn't begin with a do-gooder's social analysis of their situation; it begins with *their* assessment.

It would be easy to interpret "Feed my sheep" literally, offering only direct-service responses to the needs of low-income parishioners: food pantries, clothes closets, Catholic Charities services, and so on. But these ministries, however helpful they are, do not bring new low-income leaders into the social mission of the church. They *serve* low-income Catholics, meeting their basic needs without engaging them in social action. To draw low-income leaders into social ministry, pastoral ministers and lay leaders must first listen to the stories of low-income Catholics and then respond with encouragement to develop the skills and power to change the world as it is. This process is the true definition of *empowerment.*

Empowerment through Broad-Based Organizing

If we embraced such an empowerment approach to Jesus' instruction "Feed my sheep," we would gain an understanding of how the IAF and its constituent organizations operate. The IAF is the premier network of broad-based community organizations in the United States. Other organizing networks have built up groups that include many Catholic parishes. Space constraints prevent featuring their contributions in this chapter, but they may be operating in your backyard. These networks have alphabet-soup names like PICO, DART, and OLTC (which includes the Brockton Interfaith Community featured in Chapter 1). At least one network, Gamaliel, draws its name from scripture.

Their ability to organize gives broad-based organizations the power to negotiate effectively with those who have political and financial power. As of 2004, the IAF had fifty-five affiliates in twenty-one states, Canada, Germany, and the United Kingdom, predominantly composed of churches. In addition to improving public safety in every community in which they operate, IAF groups have worked to pass living-wage bills (Baltimore, Texas, Arizona, New York City), funded thousands of new homes for low-income workers (New York City, Philadelphia, Baltimore, Washington, DC), established the successful Alliance School System (in areas throughout the West and Southwest), and passed legislation to carry out large-scale blight removal and urban revitalization (New York City).

Some observers have criticized the IAF for thinking too small, focusing on local concerns. But IAF groups work on winnable issues, problems that are within their power. And if you are someone who shops at a store that sells rotten meat, if you live in a building where the air vents haven't been cleaned in forty years, if you live in fear in your own neighborhood, these accomplishments seem mighty indeed.

Simply put, the aim of broad-based organizing is to develop power and to act on issues identified by members as both pressing and winnable. Veteran organizer Mike Gecan explains the IAF's understanding of power:

> [The IAF] succeeds because its leaders have learned how to manufacture and manage power—the ability to act— consistently and effectively. Not the power to abuse others back. Not the power to dominate. Not the power to replace the last bully with a new bully. Not the power to keep others from entering. But the power to demand recognition and reciprocity and respect, the power to create and sustain meaningful public relationships.[2]

Who are these leaders who seek to gain and utilize power? Social justice nuts? Not-in-my-backyard types? Kooks? Crackpots? Grim do-gooders? None of these, says Gecan:

> These are normal and commonsensical people, people
> who have rich and full lives in their families and congre-
> gations and in their workplaces and communities. They
> are not activists, for the most part. They are not ideo-
> logues....They don't pledge allegiance to a single issue or
> a single leader. They don't believe a secular messiah, no
> matter how gifted or talented, can fix all that ails them.[3]

These leaders live with one foot in "the world as it is" and one foot
in "the world as it should be." They use pragmatic tactics to achieve
pragmatic results.

These tactics range from the barely audible whisper to the
flashy *60 Minutes*-style exposé. All actions, but with carefully
planned content and tone. Gecan describes one end of the tactical
spectrum through a story about East Brooklyn Congregations
(EBC) leader Alice McCollum. As an EBC delegation leader,
McCollum calmly asked the director of major construction projects
for New York City, "Sir, when do you expect to complete the renovation of Betsy Head Park and Pool?" When the official began to
filibuster, McCollum calmly interrupted, "When are you going to
repair and reopen the Park Street Pool?" The director introduced
his staff. McCollum quietly said, "I'm sorry to interrupt again, but
when do you expect to complete the renovation of Betsy Head Park
and Pool?" The official became sullen, then began screaming at the
group, and McCollum's voice dropped to a whisper, "When are you
going to repair and reopen the Park Street Pool?" No other words
were spoken by EBC leaders and clergy at the meeting. They quietly left. Days later, work crews appeared. A few months afterward,
the city reopened the renovated pool and EBC (led by McCollum)
publicly thanked the official for responding to EBC's request at a
grand reopening event.[4]

Sometimes more theatrical tactics are called for. Gecan
describes another action by the same group, in response to the rotten food, non-functioning coolers, rigged scales, and outrageous
prices of local groceries in East Brooklyn. Finding city inspectors
"woefully understaffed and basically toothless," EBC trained a group
of citizen inspectors, armed with clipboards and thermometers,
weights and measures. Teams of ten EBC inspectors entered each

store and conducted surprise inspections, taking care not to disturb other shoppers. Prior to the action EBC leaders briefed police.

One team bought "the greenest meat, the fuzziest grapes, the most rusted cans, and the hardest loaves of bread they could find." Another recorded cooler and freezer temperatures. A third group of inspectors recorded the prices of twenty preselected items for future comparison with other stores. According to Gecan: "Store managers reacted by yelling and threatening arrest. One manager tried to stop our designated shoppers from purchasing the spoiled and rotten food. 'Why do you want that stuff?' he pleaded. 'I'll get you some good food.'" After each inspection leaders presented Letters of Agreement with EBC for signature. These letters included a list of conditions that required correction. If store managers did not sign, the word would go out, in every congregation and housing project in East Brooklyn, that the store manager refused to maintain standards of cleanliness and sanitation in the store. Bigger inspection teams would return, reporters in tow, to continue the inspections. All of the targeted store managers ultimately signed the agreements, but more important, the people of East Brooklyn achieved some measure of food security.[5]

IAF tactics are not ends in themselves but means to bring about the member groups' visions of a better community. Supporting the actions of these groups is one way that the church responds to Jesus' instruction to "feed my sheep." The church feeds its flock through parish memberships in broad-based organizations, but also through the work of CCHD. Funded by an annual collection (typically the Sunday before Thanksgiving), CCHD has funded broad-based community organizing to the tune of $220 million over thirty-five years. Today, about 85 percent of the annual collection ($11 million in 2003) goes to broad-based organizing. Most organizations affiliated with the organizing networks mentioned above have received CCHD funding. Tom Chabolla, associate director of CCHD, elaborates on the reasons for this investment:

> CCHD's funding of community organizing and economic development programs is core to our mission and consistent with Catholic social teaching. When done well, community organizing helps low-income people

develop skills to benefit other aspects of parish life and ministry. Faith-based community organizing has the potential to enrich parishes by strengthening their presence in the community and making the connection between faith, worship, and life more explicit. At its best, engagement in community organizing transforms individuals and parishes alike.[6]

CCHD thus marks a collective commitment of all US bishops to the empowerment of people living in poverty, to "feed my sheep" through the development of broad-based organizing groups run by people living in poverty. This financial commitment stands in addition to the commitment of leaders within Catholic parishes, to which we now turn.

The Issue Isn't the Issue

The culture of broad-based organizing is suffused with more aphorisms than an Alcoholics Anonymous meeting. "Easy does it" and "Fake it till you make it" are replaced by "Don't do for others what they can do for themselves" and "The issue isn't the issue." The latter is the lesson, relearned with each campaign, that organizing is ultimately not about after-school programs, community policing, or affordable housing. It is about power and the development of citizen leaders.

Becoming a leader in an IAF organization is a relational process of training, action, evaluation, and action again. People enter timid yet angry, poor but possessing raw talent. Gecan describes the transformation into IAF leaders in what I would call the most successful civics classroom in America:

> When they act, as they act, people change. The poor become less poor. The disconnected of all races and classes engage. The marginalized begin to move toward the center. The powerless gather, organize, and act. Victims get their first taste of victory. At the core of the relational culture is a belief in the ability of most people

to grow and develop, as well as a faith in the newly arrived or recently organized people or formerly excluded people to exert their newfound power in effective and responsible ways.[7]

In the pages that follow we see how this process has influenced the lives of thousands, indeed millions, of New York Catholics through the stories of Catholic leaders involved in two New York City IAF groups, South Bronx Churches and Upper Manhattan Together. *Feed my sheep.*

"Watch Out for Them Church People!": Rosario Rosado and Bernard Smith

In 2001, South Bronx native Rosario Rosado returned to her childhood neighborhood after living eight years in Puerto Rico. She was shocked by what she saw:

> I was living with my aunt in New York City Housing. I saw the conditions and I said, "Oh, my God, how can people live like this? I have to do something!" But I didn't know how.
>
> Every day I would take a little piece of paper and write what I saw: graffiti, mailboxes broken, front doors not closing, elevators out of service, hallways not clean, garbage in the front of the building. Then I would go to my mother's apartment, and I would see the same thing. I asked my mother, "Don't you complain? Do you go to the housing office? Don't they do anything?" Then I said, "I'm going to do something." And she said, "You gonna get me in trouble." And I said, "No, I'm going to do something. You've been living here how long? And this is getting worse, not better."
>
> So I started writing on pieces of paper. I saw the way that the maintenance guy was cleaning up. I asked him, "Do you use soap?" He said, "No." I said, "Oh." I wrote it down.[8]

Looking for others concerned about the conditions of public housing, Rosado, a parishioner at Immaculate Conception of the Blessed Virgin Mary Church, attended a meeting of SBC, an IAF affiliate composed of eight Catholic and seventeen Protestant churches. Organizer Marielys Divanne encouraged Rosado to research the situation more systematically. She then gathered fellow tenants for a research action. Rosado describes the experience:

> We started going from the roof all the way down, writing down what we saw and taking pictures of everything. We got ready to meet with Miss Lola, our New York City Housing Authority manager. We showed her and her staff the pictures. They were surprised. I was scared. I said to myself, "I'm going to get my mother in trouble. But here goes, you gotta change. Shyness got to go."
>
> They said, "Oh, this isn't happening." We said, "Well, yes, it is. You don't live there. We live there."
>
> Slowly it's been changing. It's a big long process. We still have to keep on working. They are using soap now. My mother's building is cleaner. My mother put in a complaint not too long ago, and they came right away, where before it was months and months before they would come.[9]

Rosado speaks proudly of the changes that have occurred in New York public-housing complexes, but also about the changes she has experienced in herself. She describes herself as "quiet and shy" before joining SBC. Now she sees herself as a leader. She credits her transformation to good training, particularly the IAF ten-day national training. She explains:

> At the IAF training, they show you how to fight, but to fight in the right way. The wrong way is if I start using foul language or hitting. I won't get very far. I might get satisfaction, but I won't get what I want. The right way is talking to the person, doing our actions with the right people. If it's something legal, we do our legal work.
>
> When you come and see them they say, "Wow, this person is not playing. She really knows what she is say-

ing," so it gets done. You've got to be on top of them. That's what motivated me; I saw that I could make a difference.[10]

Rosado learned what legendary IAF organizer Ernesto Cortes has called "cold anger"—what remains when leaders "take the hot impulse of their anger and cool it down so that it can become a useful tool to improve individual lives and the quality of the common community."[11]

Bernard Smith is another "shy" leader of SBC acquainted with cold anger. He first became involved out of a sense of obligation to his children, their education, and their well-being. Skeptical in the beginning, he quickly became impressed by the accomplishments and methods of SBC. He recounts:

> When I first joined I'd say, "We're never going to get this done!" or "This is going to take forever!" I see now that it's meeting with the right people, and getting all of the churches together. Sometimes we'd get two or three hundred people out. I said, "Whoa! This is something!"
>
> And now in my apartment complex, there's a saying going around, "Watch out for them church people!" If they see church people coming, they look busy; they start scrubbing or mopping or something. Little by little, I see things getting done. One day we all came out of church and we saw a wastebasket on our corner that's never been there. But two weeks prior to that, when we met with the Department of Transportation, we asked for that. They said, "Well, you know how politics works," and this and that. When we saw that wastebasket, that little thing, some of our leaders told the other parishioners, "Look! Look! We got a wastebasket." You just don't see that in the South Bronx.[12]

Talk about the issue not being the issue! A trash can? The real issue, of course, was power. Smith, Rosado, and their fellow SBC leaders transformed the relationship between low-income citizens and an unresponsive bureaucracy by developing power and using it responsibly. That new power relationship was more important than any particular achievement and developed political capital to be expended in another campaign. Smith and SBC recently put that relationship to the test working on a children's health campaign (the child asthma rate in some neighborhoods in the Bronx is 20 percent[13]). He explains:

> Neighbors that have been in my building for thirty or forty years say that the air vents have never been cleaned. They're filthy. You don't know what's nesting up in there. We got an action together to get our air vents cleaned. Most of the kids have asthma. We don't know what they're breathing out of the air vents. We met with the director, and they cleaned the air vents in my building. Now we want to get the vents in *all* of the complexes in New York City cleaned. We're still fighting for that.[14]

Like most of the interviewees, Smith's reasons for being active in SBC changed over the years. His reasons for joining related to *his* children, *their* education, *their* health and well-being. Now he fights for the health of *all* low-income children in the five boroughs of New York City.

Rosado also underwent a similar enlargement of interest. She began working with SBC to improve conditions in her and her mother's apartment complexes. Now she fights for the dignity of everyone in the South Bronx. Rosado considers the meaning of her own life and the legacy that she will leave behind:

> No matter if it's a little piece of land that I fixed, I did something. When I pass on, I want people to remember that I was a fighter. That I said, "Don't let anyone tell you that you can't do what you could do." I want to make this place a dreamland.[15]

A dreamland? The South Bronx? Twenty years ago such a thought might have been laughable. But Rosado's success in improving her and her mother's quality of life led her to dream such dreams of new life and to see herself not as "quiet and shy," but as "a fighter." *Feed my sheep.*

"We Own the South Bronx": Felix Santiago

In 1986, Felix Santiago's pastor had a vision of the South Bronx. Only it was a nightmare. Felix's pastor said to him:

> "You must get involved now. If you do not take charge of the South Bronx now, if you do not try to own it now, you are never going to own it. Fifteen years from now, the outsiders, the developers, will come and they will take over." I said, "OK, let me try it, because it's winter and I've got nothing to do."[16]

There were times in the 1980s that Santiago wondered if the South Bronx was worth saving. He watched firefighters hose the blood off the street where St. Luke's Church stands when "seven people got shot at the same time." He saw "garbage in every corner of the street." He and his family lived in fear of the omnipresent drug trade. They considered moving to the still-affordable northern suburbs of Rockland County, but, impressed with some of SBC's initial achievements, he said, "I'll give this a chance."

SBC developed a plan centered on public-safety improvements such as community policing, food security (like EBC's supermarket actions), and, its most ambitious project, Nehemiah Homes, a redevelopment and affordable home-ownership plan to build one thousand single-family homes in the South Bronx.[17] The homes would be built on vacant lots and the sites of abandoned buildings that were being used for drugs and prostitution.

Gathering signatures for SBC's plan to renew the South Bronx in 1986, Santiago stood at the corner of Westchester Avenue and 149th street, corralling friends, neighbors, and strangers alike. He recalls:

> Some people said "What do we have to sign up for?" I said "Do you see those abandoned buildings burning over there on that hill? In a few years, you will have a house over there. A new home. We want to rebuild the South Bronx." So they said, "Well, I'll sign that."[18]

The coming years brought actions and confrontations, accountability sessions and negotiations with New York leaders who are household names nationally: Ed Koch, David Dinkins, Rudy Guiliani, John Cardinal O'Connor. In the end, SBC raised millions of dollars and built one thousand single-family homes on land donated by the City of New York. These homes are now owned by low-income working people.

Felix Santiago is one of those Nehemiah homeowners. Ten years after he stood on the corner of Westchester and 149th Street gathering signatures, he drew Nehemiah House #276 in the SBC-sponsored lottery. A visit to the construction site proved to be an emotional experience. "They were building the house," he recalls. "I went in and I looked out the window. I saw the corner where I had stood, and all of my hairs stood up."[19]

Santiago is now a homeowner, but listening to him, you would think that he owned the entire South Bronx:

> We own the community now. When we went around with the police in the van [identifying drug-dealing hotspots in the 1980s], we were kind of afraid. We thought that maybe the drug dealers were going to see us. But we were not afraid together. Everywhere we went, from New York to Albany, from Albany back to Washington, we would carry our signatures with us, and we would put them on the table and say, "These 100,000 people agree with our agenda for change."
>
> That made a big difference in our lives. We began to own more of the community. It's something you learn with South Bronx Churches. You don't fear anybody. You can stand in front of the president of the United States and you can talk to him like we are here. You have power. In 1986 I would have been afraid to sit down here and talk to you. I would say, no way, no way, you don't want to talk to me. But when you get picked to be a leader and own what you got, you have the right to represent the community.[20]

Like Rosado and Smith, Santiago grew from someone who quietly endured the crucifixion of the South Bronx into a leader helping to bring new life to his community. He now owns the South Bronx in both a literal and figurative sense. And those other 999 low-income Nehemiah homeowners are now community stakeholders who will ensure that the South Bronx grows into a safe and affordable future, perhaps a "dreamland."

Shepherd and Flock Together: Ana Jaquez, José Jimenez, and Bishop Gerald Walsh

Once burned, twice shy. It's an expression that Ana Jaquez of UMT understands. Jaquez is a thirty-year resident of the neighborhoods of northern Manhattan, those neighborhoods north of 125th Street that the tourist maps omit, like ancient maps whose edges proclaim "Here be monsters." Jaquez explains that by the time she moved to St. Elizabeth's Parish (Washington Heights), she had lost faith in community organizations:

> Quite a few people have approached me, asking for help with their organization, but I say "No way!" I'm not going to get involved because people come to our community to take advantage of us. They take advantage of the good ideas that we have, and then all of a sudden, they just disappear. Then you say, "What is going on?" They try to use you.[21]

José Jimenez, a forty-year resident of Washington Heights, is less harsh in his criticism of local community organizations, but nevertheless offers his agreement. "We had a few organizations over the years," he says, "but they didn't get much done."[22]

Enter Auxiliary Bishop Gerald Walsh, vicar of North Manhattan. In 1998, Walsh (then a monsignor) was preparing to come to St. Elizabeth's when an IAF organizer visited to explain the founding of a new regional organization, Upper Manhattan Together. Knowing about the drug markets, the lack of recreational space for youth, the conditions of the subway, and the lack of affordable housing, Walsh looked for a way to affect the community. "This group had a good track record, so I figured, 'We'll try this and see what happens,'"[23] he recalls.

Bishop Walsh invited cautious leaders like Jaquez and Jimenez to participate. They set aside their reservations when their pastor asked them to give the organization a chance. *Follow me!* Before long, UMT's accomplishments began to fuel genuine enthusiasm. It developed credibility in the community by working with police to shut down street-corner drug sales, recording rat sightings and leaning on public health authorities to respond, helping parish members utilize the Earned Income Tax Credit (EITC), and pushing New York's Metropolitan Transit Authority to make its first major repairs on the 191st Street subway station in ninety-six years.

An area jaded by experiences with some carpetbagging community organizations thus developed a mediating institution that residents could count on. Jaquez explains that it is no accident that an enduring organization grew from church leadership:

> One of the most important things is that you know you can depend on someone, so that when you explain the situation, they help you. People say, "You know who can help you? Go to St. Elizabeth's Church." But then they say, "Oh, my God, no! I don't have my papers." And people say back to them, "That's OK, you can trust them, they are not going to tell such and such." So, they trust the church, not just us, but the church.[24]

Jaquez now sees UMT as a power broker in the best sense of the word; people who had little power to affect the negative forces in their lives (drug dealers, rats, unwelcome showers in the subway station) now have a voice.

Bishop Walsh also sees positive changes in the neighborhood because of the work of UMT. But he is more proud of the leadership development that he has observed. He explains:

> They are more confident in their ability to do something. Before, they thought that because they weren't perfect English speakers, there wasn't much they could do. But that has proven to be not the case. Even if you

can't speak English, you can get with people who speak both languages, and you can get your thoughts across. And their English is not as bad as they thought it was. They're seeing now that instead of sitting back and just bemoaning stuff, they can try to do something about it, which gives them more self-confidence.[25]

From the beginning of his involvement with UMT and the IAF, Bishop Walsh has kept the "feed my sheep" of scripture in mind. He elaborates the connection of this scripture to the Eucharist:

We're feeding them, not only in the Eucharist, but also with the awareness that the Eucharist, to be complete, has to express itself in the way we live during the week. I've always told them that prayer and action go together; one isn't complete without the other. Prayer isn't complete without action to follow up on it, and action without a prayer life is going to peter out sooner or later.[26]

The experience of UMT indicates the connection between "Feed my sheep" and "Follow me!" The shepherd can indeed teach the sheep to fight off the wolves, but he must invite them to come to the planning meeting. It simply takes a good listener to invite parishioners into leadership and a mediating institution committed to developing those leaders. This person need not be the pastor but must be part of the recognized church leadership, sharing in the ministry of shepherding.

Lessons of Broad-Based Organizing: Get Out of Your Boat

The hunger that IAF leaders demonstrate for skill development, for learning how to be effective in public life, is nothing short of remarkable. Despite their experience of crucifixion (rent *Fort Apache: The Bronx* if you don't believe me), these Catholics still vow to live as Easter people. They are fed through the Eucharist, as Bishop Walsh points out, but also through the completion of the

Eucharist in public life. They build the world as it should be out of their experience of brokenness, emerging from a cocoon of shyness (which I read as low self-esteem) into the public arena.

It is an experience of new life encouraged by the US bishops through CCHD and individual pastors like Bishop Walsh, along with religious, deacons, and ecclesial lay ministers who empower the flock using the relational organizing methods explored in Chapter 1. "Follow me!" Without their initial prodding, agitation, and invitation, the flock would not be fed. Virginia Gonzalez, a SBC leader, articulates the role of church leaders in bringing low-income Catholics into social ministries, as "Follow me!" meets "Feed my sheep":

> The gospel challenges us: if you really want to walk on water, get out of your boat. Because if you stay in your boat, you might be very comfortable, you might feel safe, but you're still in your boat. That was the challenge that Jesus made to Peter. Everything comes down to action. How much can you say you love your community, love your neighbor, love your children, if you do nothing to show that love?[27]

Chapter 1's lessons of invitation return, as we note the role of church leaders in empowering low-income parishioners to take leadership in social ministry, inviting them to "get out of your boat."

We may also draw four other lessons from the church's experience with broad-based organizing. First, to engage low-income leaders in the social mission of the church, you must take the time to get to know their concerns and interests. Use the relational organizing techniques described in Chapter 1. Invite them out of the boat. Second, it is essential to connect with one of the many local, regional, or national groups that do leadership development for civic engagement. They can provide training and consulting that most parish staff and volunteer leaders cannot offer. None of the shepherds involved in broad-based organizing goes it alone; neither should you.

Third, let the leaders lead. Keep working with them on their long-term agenda, and ask them to articulate the vision of social ministry that they want to build. Challenge them, but let the low-income leaders manage the agenda. Finally, if you attend a parish mixed in terms of social class, find ways to help the middle-income and wealthier parishioners hear the stories of the low-income parishioners. You might develop your own Journey to Justice experience in the parish. The middle-income parishioners may have some professional expertise to offer, in addition to serving as allies. It is important, however, that the wealthier parishioners don't come to dominate the agenda or set the direction of the group. It is very easy for this to happen in a mixed-class group. For that reason CCHD insists that its funded groups maintain low-income leadership up to and including the level of boards of directors.

These four lessons emerge from the church's experience of empowering its low-income members in the United States through broad-based organizing. In Chapter 7 we turn from broad-based organizing to related but more specific concerns: the needs of millions of Catholic low-wage workers. *Feed my sheep*.

7

Worker Justice

In this chapter we look at a second application of Christ's *empower-ment* tool: the church's efforts to promote worker justice, exploring the work of four of today's labor priests and the lay leaders they empower. We examine their ministries for lessons to help us engage low-income Catholics in social ministry, noting that pastoral concern for low-income parishioners draws Catholic parishes into worker justice ministries, not a preexisting interest in labor on the part of the pastor. The proper relationship between church and union figures prominently in this discussion. We begin our consideration of this application of "Feed my sheep" with a frightening thought: the demise of the labor priest.

Whither Thou, Labor Priest?

The call came from a diocesan social action director in the Midwest. Did I know a labor priest who would be a good speaker for the diocese's upcoming social justice day? "No, they're all dead," I replied. Unsatisfied with my flip answer, she pressed me for more. "Could you try to find me one?" she asked. "Sure," I said, "I'll give it a try."

My calls to other national Catholic organizations proved fruitless. A Google search turned up a frightening number of memorial services. A sizable number honored Msgr. George Higgins, who in his later years served as unofficial chaplain to the labor movement. Several websites paid tribute to the recently deceased Fr. "Wild" Bill O'Donnel of the Diocese of Oakland and

Fr. Martin "Mitz" Mangan of the Diocese of Springfield (Illinois), both local legends for their actions in behalf of workers. Others honored Msgr. Clement Kern of the Archdiocese of Detroit, who founded the Association of Catholic Trade Unionists, and Jesuit Father John Corridan, played by Karl Malden in *On the Waterfront*. A few Internet sites noted retired labor priests such as Msgr. Charles Owen Rice of the Diocese of Pittsburgh, whose *Fighter with a Heart: Writings of Charles Owen Rice* (1996) ought to be read widely.

Finding no active labor priests, I asked Kim Bobo, executive director of Interfaith Worker Justice and a few members of The Roundtable Association of Diocesan Social Action Directors the less inflated question, "Do you know some priests who are doing good work on behalf of and with low-wage workers?" I gathered four names from different areas of the country. The speed at which I found these twenty-first-century labor priests with the latter question evoked the Mark Twain quip, "Rumors of my death have been greatly exaggerated!"

Through interviews with each of the four I learned that today's labor priests are different from their twentieth-century predecessors, mainly because the priesthood itself has changed. Pastoring a parish is job number one for them, a complex set of tasks and roles they increasingly take on by themselves and with the help of women religious, deacons, and lay ecclesial ministers. Today's pastor can't afford to focus on any single issue because the needs of his flock are so disparate.

Yet these four priests placed worker justice high on the list of parish priorities. Why? "Feed my sheep." The needs of the flock draw them into worker justice issues. In the process of responding to these needs, twenty-first century labor priests invite low-income parishioners into social ministry, helping them develop leadership skills for public life through participation in parish actions, worker associations, and unions. Today's labor priests and the lay leaders they develop teach us lessons about engaging low-income parishioners in social action. In the rest of this chapter we look at brief profiles of these four contemporary labor priests, with an extended look at one parish and its success in engaging low-income Catholics in social action ministries. As you read these stories, ask yourself if they are the stories of your parish or of a subgroup within your parish. How will you respond? *Feed my sheep.*

Fr. Damian Zuerlein, Archdiocese of Omaha

Fr. Damian Zuerlein insists that he didn't go looking for the designation labor priest. "I had no great desire for social justice work," he recounts. "I just wanted to live and work with the poor." A priest of the Archdiocese of Omaha, Zuerlein became involved in worker justice issues at Our Lady of Guadalupe Parish in the heart of Omaha's meatpacking district. One Sunday Mass, early in his tenure, he noticed that some parishioners did not participate in the Sign of Peace. Why? Upon inquiry he learned that most of those avoiding hand contact had developed Carpal Tunnel Syndrome or lost fingers through their jobs in the meatpacking plants. He also learned that termination was the usual outcome of such work-place injuries.

Zuerlein explains that hearing the stories of these parishioners changed him and his understanding of the role of a pastor. "Sometimes the role of shepherd is to console," he said. "But sometimes it is to protect your sheep. There are wolves out there." He met with meatpacking workers throughout the parish and learned of unpaid overtime pay, capricious termination and promotion policies, and infrequent bathroom breaks. Through Our Lady of Guadalupe's participation in Omaha Together—One Community (OTOC), another IAF broad-based organization, the parish hired an organizer to develop a meatpacking workers' association.

One of the first actions of OTOC was a health study of workers in each of Omaha's meatpacking plants. This effort included classes on worker rights led by the Occupational Safety and Health Administration (OSHA) and human rights lawyers. OTOC also joined forces with the United Food and Commercial Workers (UFCW) to try to unionize many of the plants. Several hard-fought battles resulted in increased wages, widened health coverage, the establishment of a sick-day benefit, and amendment of the family-leave policy to allow workers to return to Mexico for funerals. Many of the workers formed UFCW locals, but questions (and tensions) linger about the role of OTOC in those now unionized plants.

"Once the union election was held, I think they expected us to go away," explains Zuerlein. "But unions have forgotten how to

organize, and they don't know how to organize immigrant workers." Zuerlein remains confident that the relationship between
OTOC, with its broad-based organizing approach, and the UFCW
can continue to grow and mature. He characterizes continued discussions among high-level leaders of the organizations as promis-
ing and insists that, despite some bumps in the road, collaboration
between organized labor and organized Catholics is essential to
bringing about justice for meatpacking workers.[1]

Fr. Brendan Curran, OP,
Archdiocese of Chicago

Dominican father Brendan Curran has a hard time sitting still
when people are hurting. "What do we clergy do when people tell
us about the challenges they face?" he asks. "I find it difficult to
function if I just sit with people's stories and don't do something."

"You mention something in a homily," he explains, "and
people want to talk about it afterwards." In his work as associate pastor at St. Pius V parish in Chicago, Fr. Curran has come face to face
with the economic and social problems that confront the faithful.
Some parishioners worry about their survival as they float from job
to job. Others express concern as their children become involved in
street violence. Many talk about routine abuses on the job, such as
firings when workers become eligible for retirement benefits.

In the summer of 2001 an issue emerged that affected hundreds of St. Pius parishioners. The US Social Security Administration began sending "no match" letters to employers and employees
in cases where Social Security numbers appeared to be incorrectly
applied. The "no match" program was intended to see that workers received proper credit for their earnings—a problem if a name
and Social Security number don't match the Social Security
Administration's records. A discrepancy can occur for a number of
reasons, and these letters specifically stated that they should not be
used by employers as grounds to fire employees. But many employers used the letters to intimidate, harass, and fire workers, particularly those outspoken about abuses or involved in efforts to organize.

The 9/11 attacks only accelerated the "no match" program, as
homeland security leaders expanded it into an anti-terrorism meas-

ure. Responding to increasing reports of intimidation and firings, Curran organized a "town hall" meeting with other concerned clergy. St. Pius V Church hosted the event, which featured a dialogue with the regional commissioner for Social Security (one of twelve nationwide). Curran reports that the commissioner was shocked to see five hundred hands shoot into the air when he asked, "How many people have been threatened with firing because of these letters?" As a result of this meeting and continued dialogue, Chicago's regional SSA commissioner became outspoken on behalf of workers harmed by employers taking illegal actions based on these letters.

The work on "no match" letters has continued for Curran. In 2004 parishioners asked him to intervene as an "interpreter" in a case of seventy-five hotel workers who faced immediate termination after receiving "no match" letters. Working with a union representing workers from the hotel's parent corporation and high-level managers from the company, Fr. Curran and his parishioners were able to reverse the hotel's policy of immediate termination of employees receiving "no match" letters.[2]

Fr. Edward Byrne, Archdiocese of New York

Fr. Edward Byrne of St. Ann Parish, Ossining, in New York's Westchester County, was surprised at the number of young Ecuadorian men who began coming to Mass during the year 2000. Where did they come from? What did they do for work? What were their needs? He asked a staff member to call a meeting after Mass of the Hispanic congregation. Not one parishioner attended. How do I make a connection with this large and growing part of my church? he wondered.

Then a young man came for help. Like many other St. Ann's parishioners, he was a day laborer, working at construction sites, private homes, and on other manual work crews. At one site, after a dispute with workers, the owner refused to pay them wages owed, took their (company) jackets, and made the workers walk ten miles home in the chilly fall air. Byrne called the owner, who in turn threatened to call the police (many day laborers are in the country illegally). "Great, I'm the police chaplain," replied Fr. Byrne. Bringing together area ministers and two parish lawyers, Fr. Byrne and his colleagues took the owner to small claims court and earned a three-quarters settlement, persevering despite a $50,000 libel lawsuit filed by the owner.

Many other Ecuadorian men came forward. The practice of defrauding undocumented immigrant day workers was widespread. Fr. Byrne expanded the ad hoc group into a city-wide organization, the Hispanic Employee Labor Project (HELP). Composed of six priests and ministers, one rabbi, and a score of lay leaders, HELP has obtained payment for over one hundred Hispanic workers whose wages were wrongfully withheld. In many cases a letter from HELP has been enough to motivate employers to pay workers. A large number of other cases ended with small-claims-court settlements.

One particularly egregious case resulted in New York Attorney General Elliot Spitzer freezing an employer's assets until the offending individual paid the small-claims-court judgment. Fr. Byrne has since invited local police to speak at the parish about the rights of workers to payment of earned wages and freedom from assault. His work demonstrates that law-enforcement officials can be important allies to groups promoting justice for workers, even undocumented workers.[3]

Developing Lay Leaders

In each of these parishes the needs of the flock drew the shepherds into action for justice. In turn, the priests then drew parishioners from that flock into leadership roles. A worker justice campaign affords many opportunities for the development of low-income leaders. Who speaks for the workers at meetings and actions? Who runs for offices within the unions and worker associations? Who sits at the negotiating table?

Fathers Zuerlein, Curran, and Byrne selected and developed the lay leaders who took on these roles. Some have argued that the labor priest has been replaced by laity who put their faith into action through unions and worker associations. I think they are half right. Members of the laity lead most organizations for worker justice, but the shepherds still feed the flock. These three labor priests demonstrate the impact a parish can make when parish leaders invite low-income Catholics into social ministry based on their experience of economic injustice. The fourth, Fr. Michael Gutierrez of the Archdiocese of Los Angeles, teaches us what can happen when action for worker justice becomes the focal ministry of an entire parish.

Fr. Michael Gutierrez, Archdiocese of Los Angeles

St. Anne's Church in Santa Monica, California, lies in the shadow of St. Monica's, church of the stars, where Governor Arnold Schwarzenegger and First Lady Maria Shriver worship, along with untold actors and would-be actors. Starbucks locations are more abundant than ATMs in this neighborhood. Casual gourmet eateries abound, as well as upscale clothing boutiques, tourist hotels, and trendy bars. Two kinds of Catholics live in this area: Anglos, who spend money in these service-sector establishments and attend St. Monica's, and Hispanics, who work for these employers and attend St. Anne's.

On the day following Pope John Paul II's death, Fr. Michael Gutierrez, pastor of St. Anne's preaches a homily in tribute to the late pontiff. "Behind every great labor leader is a great priest," he begins, as he tells the familiar story of Pope John Paul II's friendship with Solidarity leader Lech Walesa. With great excitement he reviews the pope's role in energizing the Solidarity labor movement, and Walesa's ascension to the presidency of Poland. Gutierrez explains that the pope's commitment to worker justice represents a Catholic tradition, a tradition that St. Anne's continues to embody through its efforts to promote worker justice. These efforts include the parish's support of workers involved in unions, its work to promote living-wage legislation with interfaith partner Clergy and Laity United for Economic Justice (CLUE), and its encouragement of youth anti-sweatshop activities.[4]

Later that day Gutierrez elaborates on why he calls himself a John Paul II priest:

> I remember seeing one of those papal Masses as a kid, and they had the Solidarity signs going up in the air all during Mass. Then I read *Laborem exercens* in high

school. It made sense to me. John Paul gave a very clear message early on. He was always a worker rights activist. He was the model of what we are supposed to be doing, to be a pastoral leaven.[5]

Gutierrez sees the parish's focus on worker justice as "applied pastoral theology," the application of faith principles to the realities of parishioner's lives. "If it's a strike, it's solidarity; if it's the loss of a job, it's support of them and their families; if they are sick, you go to the hospital and visit with them. It's everything that our people struggle with."[6] *Feed my sheep.*

In a parish comprised of low-wage workers, most of the pastoral concerns ultimately return to a lack of money. The lack of affordable housing also creates financial strains for families. Absent parents working three jobs leave children and teens unsupervised, suggesting that many youth problems are economic issues. Their lack of money also leaves individual parishioners without much of a voice in public life.

In response to these pastoral issues, Gutierrez began working with union members in the parish and union leaders outside of it. He got the parish involved in the living-wage advocacy of CLUE, a push to raise the city minimum wage to $10.50 an hour. Many of his homilies began to address worker justice issues like wages and benefits, working conditions, and union representation. He recalls that, in the beginning, not all parishioners were supportive. "Some older parishioners in the Spanish-speaking congregation and some school parents were upset when we started talking about worker issues," he explains. "But I said, 'Just remember what John Paul did in the 1980s. He went to Poland and told Solidarity members to stand fast!'"

Today, Gutierrez gets a nasty letter when he does *not* preach on social justice. "I just got a three-page letter from someone who was disappointed because one Sunday I preached on the Rosary instead of 'real issues,'"[7] he says incredulously. The parish has become a hotbed of worker activism, from participation in unions to legislative advocacy to anti-sweatshop work. But these activities did not begin at Gutierrez's behest. Rather, they started much as HELP did in St. Ann's Parish in Ossining, New York, when a parishioner came forward, asking for help. *Feed my sheep.*

Supporting and Confronting Unions

Fr. Gutierrez credits parishioner Jose Sanchez with drawing him into efforts for worker justice. The food-service worker at UCLA Medical Center, the largest employer in the parish, believed that a pattern of harassment had emerged against workers who became leaders in his union, AFSCME Local #3299. When a co-worker received a disciplinary warning for refusing to clean the food-service kitchen using harsh chemicals without proper protection, Sanchez planned to attend a union demonstration on the worker's behalf. He invited Fr. Gutierrez.[8] The successful demonstration led to greater protections for UCLA kitchen workers, but it also introduced Gutierrez to the union's activities and began a relationship of both support and confrontation.

The relationship between St. Anne's and AFSCME has drawn the parish and its interfaith ally CLUE into specific union concerns. For example, when AFSCME discovered that the ratio of patients to nurses in intensive care was 11:1 rather than 6:1, as required by state law, a religious delegation led by Gutierrez met with the hospital's patient-relations department to discuss the situation.

More recently, the parish has been preparing for a strike at UCLA Medical Center. After two years without any pay raises for workers, the union convinced management to agree to a 2 percent worker raise in 2004. Then the management team at the hospital changed. The new administration announced that there were to be no raises, after all. Today hospital management insists that the center's financial condition has become so precarious that raises are no longer an option. But Irene Santiago, a parishioner and house-keeping worker active in strike preparations, notes, "They gave raises to the nurses, but they didn't give it to us in housekeeping, or in the kitchen."[9] Curiously, the new management team found the funds to keep its promises to one class of workers but not another.

Fr. Gutierrez explains how the church should respond to such a situation:

> The role of the church in our case is to make sure that the workers are heard. So it's a matter now where we will do delegation work with the leadership of the hospital, and say, "Hey, you promised but you didn't deliver. You

need to keep your promises. The union didn't say that you are bad people; you just didn't keep your promise."[10]

He also points out the importance of reaching out to UCLA students, enlisting them as allies, as well as making contact with Catholics and other people of faith within the UCLA administration.

When Santiago relates the story of a co-worker whose supervisor told her that all striking UCLA workers would be fired, Gutierrez interrupts. "That's where the church has to step in and remind them, 'You have that right. Nobody can say that to you. It's the law of the State of California.'" He turns to Santiago and says, "If you've got the name of that supervisor, I'd love to hand it in."[11]

During the Safeway Supermarket strike of 2004, St. Anne's Parish was especially active. Scores of parishioners walked the picket lines, and the parish provided money for food and rent for needy union families. Cynthia Garcia, the wife of a grocery worker who went on strike, notes that while many families appreciated the thousands of dollars in aid provided by the parish, "Fr. Mike's homilies were the most helpful." She adds, "He compared the carrying of the grocery workers picket signs to Jesus carrying the cross."[12] Gutierrez and other prominent parishioners walked the picket lines as a show of solidarity with grocery workers. He also participated in a CLUE meeting between striking grocery workers and the Safeway CEO. The strike changed how parishioners shopped, and despite no real improvement in wages or benefits at Safeway, contracts favorable to workers were quickly signed by other grocery chains across the country, after they measured the full impact of the strike.

The grocery strike also demonstrated that relations between parishioners and their unions are not always sanguine. Gutierrez points out that as important as supporting unions is, sometimes the role of the church is to confront a union:

When it comes down to workers' rights, the church is definitely on the side of the worker. There is no choice there. We respect the unions, but sometimes we have to push back at the union because we have to protect the worker. During the supermarket strike we did that. The supermarket strike was started by the unions. They took on a major corporation with no game plan, and for the first two months they were getting beaten. And there was no major clergy support, because they didn't talk to us. After a couple of months union leadership started listening to clergy. Our advice was "Listen to your workers" [who suggested ending the strike before it had even more devastating effects on their families].[13]

Gutierrez maintains that he has intervened with unions on behalf of parish members on numerous occasions. Often, it is because a particular grievance does not get the attention that the worker believes it deserves or a worker is told to wait for a concern to be addressed. He explains:

I understand the union's point at times. But I have to say to union leaders, "We're here for the worker." We intercede for workers and say, "Hey, you need to consider it. You can't just say, 'Hey, he's complaining.' Well of course he's complaining. You promised to be the one who was going to be a voice for him!"[14]

The church therefore acts as a mediating institution between worker and union as well as between worker and employer. At the same time, Gutierrez works to develop the union members within the parish to organize others to support union activities. It is a balancing act that begins and ends with the principle that the church's role is to help low-wage workers live lives of dignity. Often that means challenging employers, but it can also mean challenging unions.

Families for a Living Wage

St. Anne's Church supports many unionized workers within the parish, but it also engages families who do not belong to unions in efforts for worker justice. One such family is the Jaras. As a teenager, Ana G. Jara was active in public life, opposing California's anti-immigrant proposition 187, but the church was not part of her activism. "I had fallen away," she recalls. In 1999, she took a course on liberation theology at UCLA and "learned how to connect my spiritual life with my community involvement." At about the same time, the Archdiocese of Los Angeles assigned Fr. Michael Gutierrez to her home parish, St. Anne's. Attending Mass again for the first time in six years, she liked what she heard from the pulpit. "I started talking to my family about it, and convinced them to come to church. I was really convinced that things were moving there."[15]

Ana's mother, Ana Maria Jara, and younger sister, Christina Lizama, also took a closer look at St. Anne's Parish. They became passionately involved in the parish's collaboration with CLUE to promote living-wage legislation. If you ask parishioners like the Jaras why they embrace the living-wage issue, they will offer a strikingly conservative answer. "Kids should spend more time with their parents," states Ana Maria Jara. "If their parents don't have a living wage, they'll have to work two or three different jobs, and that keeps the children on their own."[16] The Jaras and other parishioners at St. Anne's are not advocating for a big government program; they want to promote family values.

The Jara family first stepped into CLUE's living-wage campaign when Ana G. Jara attended a rally in April 2000 to encourage the Santa Monica City Council to pass a living-wage ($10.50/hour) ordinance. This ordinance was slated to raise dramatically the minimum wage in Santa Monica and did not pass without controversy. Fr. Gutierrez invited Ana G. to the April rally and asked her to become involved in the planning with CLUE. She talks about her first meeting:

> Fr. Mike said, "You know, I'd really like you to come on board, and just learn and experience this thing." So I thought I'd be going to meetings and just listening and learning more. But by the second meeting they had appointed me the youth liaison, and I was the one who was going to bring all of the youth to the protests. Through that work and talking to people of all different faiths, sitting down and talking to the hotel workers themselves and hearing firsthand their real needs and how living wages and health benefits and shift changes can impact a person's life sold me on getting involved with workers.[17]

The ordinance soon passed the Santa Monica City Council, but the hotel industry fought back. Hiring professional signature gatherers at a cost of twenty dollars a signature, they successfully placed a statewide referendum question designed to overturn the Santa Monica living wage on the fall 2002 California ballot.

During the referendum campaign St. Anne's parishioners got a boost when Cardinal Roger Mahony attended the St. Anne's novena in 2002. The annual novena is a tradition stretching back ninety years. Unexpectedly, Cardinal Mahony strongly endorsed the living-wage campaign in his homily, energizing the parish for the fight ahead. After a campaign described by parishioners as "full of lies," the ordinance was overturned by seven hundred votes. Uncowed by this loss, in 2004 St. Anne's and CLUE successfully persuaded the Santa Monica City Council to pass a second living-wage ordinance (now $11.50/hour) covering only city workers, a partial victory. Incidentally, the St. Anne's finance council passed a living-wage ordinance of its own in 2000, to cover parish workers. Not bad for a "poor" parish.

What is striking about the living-wage campaign is not the tumultuous see-saw of victory-defeat-victory, but the development of new leaders like the Jaras. *Feed my sheep.* The living-wage campaign was not simply a matter of Fr. Gutierrez lending a Catholic collar to CLUE's interfaith actions. It was a concerted effort to develop new parish leaders to act for justice. That required Gutierrez's efforts to get to know parishioners and then invite them in based on their interests. *Follow me!*

Developing leadership skills among parishioners is, as we observed in the previous chapter, one way of feeding the flock. Today, Ana G. Jara is a full-time worker at the Pico Family and Youth Center in Santa Monica. She is working with a cadre of youth, mentoring them, and finding ways of taking action on the issues that most concern young people. At twenty-five she teaches high school students how to meet with city council members and express their visions and concrete proposals for the city. Her mother, Ana Maria, now serves on the board of the living-wage campaign and recently ran for the school board. Dozens of leaders within the unions and CLUE have arisen through St. Anne's

Church, thanks to Gutierrez's commitment to enlarge the church's action for worker justice beyond the labor priest. *Feed my sheep.*

"If You Get the Kids, You Get the Parents."

The Jaras are illustrative of leadership development at St. Anne's for a second reason. They represent a strategy of reaching adult leaders through their children. This approach has a doubling effect. If, as Gutierrez believes, "you get the kids, you get the parents,"[18] then at least two or maybe three leaders come into the social mission of the church through recruiting efforts aimed at youth.

Watching the thirty-eight-year-old priest interact with teens, it is obvious that youth ministry is one of Gutierrez's charisms. However, much of the youth work he delegates to St. Anne's youth minister, Annie Gomba. Gomba views social justice as integral to youth ministry, helping teens "understand the times in which they are living"[19] within the context of parish traditions. For example, a *posada* is a nine-day reenactment, popular with Mexican and Mexican American Catholics, of the travels and travails of Mary and Joseph on their way to Bethlehem. This tradition has become a popular vehicle for social justice education at St. Anne's.

In 2001 *posadas* began to address social justice issues identified by parish youth. First, immigrant rights themes appeared in the reenactments. Then, in 2003, the youth took on what Fr. Gutierrez describes as "racial profiling and police harassment of young black and brown men." The youth "went to the public safety building and used it as a symbol for one of the inns that wouldn't let Mary and Joseph in. These were our best kids academically and the most active in church. They felt shut out by the police."[20] From Santa Monica's public-safety building, the youth walked to the hotel across the street to tie the *posada* back to workers rights, suggesting that the hotels deny workers full human dignity when they do not pay living wages. In Advent 2004 the *Los Angeles Times* covered a St. Anne's *posada* featuring many of these themes.

St. Anne's *posadas* did more than educate parish youth. They served as actions during the living-wage campaign that drew in parents as well as young people. In addition, the *posadas* led to an ongoing dialogue with police about the racial profiling of young Latino men. Viviana and Yvonne Villegas, two teens active in the parish youth group, believe that their conversations with police have been somewhat effective, but only the boys actively involved in the dialogue have seen a reduction in profiling.[21] The Villegas sisters say that the police learn that these young men are good students and leave them alone, but the harassment of others continues.[22]

With the support and encouragement of parish leaders, the Villegas sisters joined the Pico Youth and Family Center's education activities against sweatshops. The teens also supported striking supermarket workers by making picket signs and attending solidarity rallies through the youth center. The youth see no division between their parish life and activities at the secular youth center. "We're all Catholic there. We see each other at church," they explain. "Father knows what we do, and he supports us."

Indeed, Fr. Gutierrez and parish leaders like Ana G. Jara deserve much of the credit for the youth center's worker justice activities and the number of youth at the center who have become active in anti-sweatshop, anti-profiling, and pro-living-wage activities. They have developed a human development model that turns the "leaders of tomorrow" into leaders today, while in the process drawing in some of their parents. *Feed my sheep.*

Beyond the Labor Priest: Lessons for Social Ministry

Don't let this chapter's focus on the labor priest mislead you. You need not be a priest to engage low-wage workers in social ministry. Twentieth-century church history may be rife with labor priests, but the twenty-first-century outlook for ministry with low-wage workers promises to be increasingly led by laity and the diaconate.

Indeed, Deacon Raul Molina at St. Anne's Parish in Santa Monica suggests that among the ordained, deacons are uniquely qualified to respond to low-wage workers because they tend to have decades of experience in the work force. "You understand them because you have come from some of the same places that they have," he says. "Let's say they are janitors. I was a janitor. I was working in medical offices, cleaning at night." Deacon Molina has played an important role in developing St. Anne's worker justice ministries. When members of the St. Anne's Our Lady of Guadalupe Society approached him about "doing more than praying and cooking," he sent the society's leaders to CLUE organizing training and put them in charge of mobilization for living-wage actions, "because action is prayer."[23]

Lay ecclesial ministers and the lay leaders who typically lead social concerns committees share the deacon's personal experience of the world of work. This experience gives them a kind of solidarity with workers that priests ordained at twenty-five[24] are less likely to have. The labor priests featured in this chapter enjoy a great deal of support from lay leaders, women religious, and deacons in their parishes. It may be true, as Fr. Gutierrez says, that "behind every great labor leader there's a priest," but behind today's labor priest stand increasing numbers of parish leaders. No matter what one's role in the church, the church's ministry with low-income workers provides opportunities to engage low-income Catholics in social ministry around the issues that concern them most.

The lessons that these stories of labor priests and their parishes provide are strikingly similar to the lessons of broad-based organizing explored in Chapter 6. I note four. First, listen to the flock. Ask questions about their lives, their joys, and their frustrations. What if Fr. Zuerlein had not asked parishioners why they did not participate in the Sign of Peace at Mass? Sometimes the parishioners will come to you, as in the cases of Fathers Curran, Byrne, and Gutierrez. The key is listening to get a sense of the needs of parishioners.

Second, provide low-income leaders with organizing training, so that they may learn to speak for themselves and organize others. The labor priest and his counterparts in parish ministry simply can't go it alone, taking all responsibility for worker justice themselves. Not only is it a poor feeding of the flock, it's downright impossible. One aspect of "Feed my sheep" is inviting low-income workers to tell their stories at actions and meetings and helping them to develop the organizing skills to mobilize others to support worker justice.

Third, get to know local labor leaders. It is vital to build relationships between the two mediating institutions of church and organized labor. Sometimes these institutions are all a worker has in the rough-and-tumble world of the global economy. If you have qualms about getting involved with unions, remember the relationship between church and union is not one of blind support. The church is called to support unions when they help low-income workers and to challenge them when they do not.

Finally, seek out interfaith allies. Who are other religious leaders concerned about worker justice? Is there an Interfaith Worker Justice affiliate in your community?[25] All of the Abrahamic religions (Jewish-Christian-Muslim) recognize the importance of worker justice. Our shared scriptures even document one of the first recorded labor disputes, the Israelites' demand that Pharaoh grant them religious holidays (Exod 5). Working across religious lines can only increase your effectiveness.

These four lessons are the key elements of wisdom offered by today's labor priests and the religious, deacons, ecclesial lay ministers, and parish leaders who work with them. Far from being an endangered species, labor priests are alive and well, integrating the spirit of Vatican II into their ministries while engaging low-income Catholics in social ministry through their parishes and other mediating institutions such as unions. Their examples provide both inspiration and practical applications to help us better engage low-income Catholics in the church's social ministry. *Feed my sheep.*

Conclusion

Are You Talkin' about JESUS?

How do we engage new leaders in the social mission of the church? Bishop Schmitt's original question continues to haunt me, as it is the central problem of Catholic social ministry. The middle pew is vast, but where are the nets bursting with fish? In these pages we have located best practices in social ministry and parsed them for leadership-development lessons. The common thread, we have found, is the organizing methodology of Christ himself. I'm talkin' about JESUS! When we utilize Jesus organizing tools—invitation, conversion, and empowerment—we begin to answer the question, developing passionate disciples of Jesus Christ who act for justice in the public arena, not bitter Berthas or grim do-gooders. In this concluding chapter we look at some ways to implement these lessons in your parish.

At the Church of St. Patrick in Newburgh, New York, cables suspend a giant crown of thorns fifteen feet above the altar. The crown measures eight feet in diameter. Each thorn is eighteen inches long. For five years I have walked this communion line, looking first absently, then intently at the crown, growing to appreciate its horrible but triumphant beauty, recalling those lines from Matthew 25: "Just as you did it to one of the least of these who are members of my family, you did it to me."

It is my last Sunday Mass at St. Patrick's. Kathleen and I are migrating south with our two young daughters to New Jersey in search of shorter commutes. I am standing in line for communion, and my mind wanders. I ask myself if there a systematic way to express what the ministries profiled in this book teach us, other than shouting, "I'm talkin' about JESUS!"? Perhaps this simple list of questions will serve as a modest tool to begin to apply the organizing methodology of Jesus (invitation, conversion, and empowerment) to social ministry in your parish:

- How will you use 1–1 relational meetings and Jesus' tool of invitation to draw new leaders into social ministry in your parish? Name five people with whom you will meet during the next month.
- In your parish's direct-service ministries, are you talkin' about JESUS? How do you discuss your encounters with Christ? If you do not, how will you regularly integrate such reflection to promote conversion?
- How will you provide parishioners with more conversion experiences, that is, opportunities to meet Jesus Christ in poor and vulnerable people? Which of the specific applications of conversion in this book (JustFaith, Journey to Justice, reverse mission, service-learning) energizes you the most? Why?
- When you reflect on the lives of low-income parishioners in your church and the phrase "Feed my sheep," what comes to mind? Meet with five low-income parish leaders during the next month and ask them to name three aspects of their lives that they would change if they had the power. Which of the specific applications of empowerment (broad-based organizing, worker justice) energizes you the most? Why?

These questions are not meant to burden you or to make you feel guilty or inadequate. The aim is to organize the main ideas of this book in a handy format. Even this brief set of questions can be boiled down to one: Are you talkin' about JESUS? That is the question that sums up this book. If you answer yes, you will draw in new leaders. If you answer no, you will not.

Now, where to start? I suggest that you think back to when you felt the most energy when reading this book. One of the mantras of community organizing is "Go where the energy is." That is the place to begin in your parish. When did you feel passionate reading this book? Was it the chapter on youth? Global solidarity? Broad-based organizing? Pay attention to these cues. God may be telling you something.

I move a few steps forward in the communion line. The crown of thorns looms closer. I see how sharp the points of the thorns are, and I think of Felix Santiago of South Bronx Churches. He points up at burning buildings on a hill in the South Bronx and says to a neighbor, "In a few years, you will have a house over there. A new home." What kind of outrageous hope is this? Outrageous as Paula Snow, the cafeteria lady, negotiating with Brockton's Super-intendent of Schools over the school budget. Outrageous as JustFaith graduates like Tom Walsh dramatically simplifying their lifestyles, moving into smaller homes, and giving the money saved to anti-poverty advocacy groups. Outrageous as Kathleen Stephens, disabled with fibromyalgia and osteoarthritis getting off her middle-pew stretcher and fighting for health care for low-income people. Outrageous as Dr. Vic Trinkus watching Christ smiling at him in a Bolivian doorway, crying "My Lord and my God," and becoming medical director of Partnership in Mission. Outrageous as Maryland teenagers enlightening state legislators about the causes of homelessness. Outrageous as the low-income workers who attend Santa Monica's Church of St. Anne asserting that human dignity demands a minimum wage of $11.50 an hour. Outrageous as the resurrection. Thomas, are you listening? Other disciples encounter the audacious hope of these brothers and sisters in Christ and say, "I'll have what they're having!" Their hope and courage are contagious; their stories are, quite simply, the good news. For many new leaders the encounter with social ministry thus becomes the evangelizing moment of moments. Our role is to spread the news, to share the secret, to become evangelists. That is how we answer the riddle of the middle pew, evangelizing using Jesus' tools. Perhaps not shouting above the din of a subway sta-tion, but in our own way, in our own place and time talkin' about JESUS!

I take a final step forward and cup my hands.

"The body of Christ."

"Amen."

Notes

Introduction

1. Margaret Roach, interview by Andy Rivas, July 27, 2004.

2. Another useful social justice toolbox is that offered by the United States Conference of Catholic Bishops (USCCB), available from USCCB Publishing.

1. The Social Concerns Committee That Works

1. United States Conference of Catholic Bishops (USCCB), *Communities of Salt and Light* (Washington, DC: United States Conference of Catholic Bishops, 1993), 4. (Hereafter cited in text.)

2. An excellent resource for best practices, continuing education, and fellowship in parish social ministry is the Parish Social Ministry section of the Catholic Charities USA website.

3. Synod of Bishops, *Justice in the World* (1971), no. 6.

4. Edward T. Chambers, *Roots for Radicals* (New York: Continuum, 2003), 48.

5. Mary Beth Rogers, *Cold Anger: A Story of Faith and Power Politics* (Denton: Univ. of North Texas Press, 1990), 10.

2. The JustFaith Phenomenon

1. Ed Cortas, JustFaith testimonial, http://www.catholic charitiesusa.org/justfaith/what/testimonies.cfm.

2. Clarice Stuart, interview with Jeffry Odell Korgen, September 13, 2004.

3. Tim McCarthy, interview with Jeffry Odell Korgen, September 20, 2004.

4. Maxine Hake, interview with Jeffry Odell Korgen, September, 23, 2004.

5. Sr. Patricia Lamb, interview with Jeffry Odell Korgen, September, 15, 2004. Note that Sr. Lamb candidly acknowledged her own prejudices ("he's very conservative"); we should do the same. My experience is that labels like liberal and conservative, for example, never capture the full story; instead, they impede our effectiveness. Engaging new leaders in Catholic social ministry demands that we offer more listening and less labeling than we do currently.

6. Fr. Timothy Taugher, interview with Jeffry Odell Korgen, October 3, 2004.

7. Thomas Walsh, interview with Jeffry Odell Korgen, September 10, 2004.

8. Lucio Caruso, interview with Jeffry Odell Korgen, September 21, 2004.

9. Jack Jezreel, interview with Jeffry Odell Korgen, August 17, 2004.

10. Ibid.

11. The late founder of The Roundtable Association of Diocesan Social Action Directors, Harry Fagan, was fond of saying, "Nobody likes a grim do-gooder."

12. Caruso, interview.

13. Jezreel, interview.

14. Dr. Stephen Colecchi, interview with Jeffry Odell Korgen, November 5, 2004.

15. Ibid.

16. Jezreel, interview.

17. Valerie Schultz, "We Serve Food Not Faith," *America* (October 29, 2001), 6.

18. Although no one seems to have documented where and when Margaret Mead actually spoke these words, they are attributed to her in many popular sources.

3. A Journey to Justice

1. According to the Journey to Justice facilitator's manual, empowerment "is a process of engagement that increases the ability of individuals, families, organizations and communities to build mutually respectful relationships and bring fundamental, positive change in the conditions affecting their daily lives."

2. See Peter Henriot and Joe Holland, *Social Analysis: Linking Faith and Justice* (Maryknoll, NY: Orbis Books, 1986).

3. Rita Waldref, interview with Jeffry Odell Korgen, December 15, 2004.

4. Anita Chlipala, interview with Jeffry Odell Korgen, December 29, 2004.

5. John P. Hogan, *Credible Signs of Christ Alive: Case Studies from the Catholic Campaign for Human Development* (Lanham, MD: Sheed and Ward, 2003), 68.

6. Marjorie O'Sullivan, interview with Jeffry Odell Korgen, December 20, 2004.

7. Waldref, interview.

8. Kathleen Stephens, interview with Jeffry Odell Korgen, December 26, 2004.

9. Ibid.

10. O'Sullivan, interview.

11. Ibid.

12. Created by Tom Turner of the Bishop Sullivan Center of the Diocese of Kansas City–St. Joseph, That's Not Fair is a faith-and-citizenship program designed to help sixth- and seventh-grade students learn about Catholic social teaching and legislative advocacy. For more information, see the bishopsullivan.org website.

13. O'Sullivan, interview.

14. Nora Dvorak, interview with Jeffry Odell Korgen, December 29, 2004.

15. Jim Moran, interview with Jeffry Odell Korgen, December 29, 2004.

16. Dan Ebener, interview with Jeffry Odell Korgen, January 28, 2005.

4. Global Solidarity and the Middle Pew

1. Maria Nordone, interview with Jeffry Odell Korgen, December 28, 2004.

2. Maria Nordone, quoted in Mustard Seed Communities USA, *Work the Word* (Mahwah, NJ: Paulist Press, 2005), 23.

3. Art Sheridan, interview with Jeffry Odell Korgen, January 8, 2005.

4. Ibid.

5. Ibid.

6. Fr. Gregory Ramkissoon, interview with Jeffry Odell Korgen, January 8, 2005.

7. Ibid.

8. Ibid.

9. Ibid.

10. Ibid.

11. Thomas Garlitz, interview with Jeffry Odell Korgen, January 5, 2005.

12. Ibid.

13. Doug Casper, interview with Jeffry Odell Korgen, January 2, 2005.

14. Dr. Vic Trinkus, interview with Jeffry Odell Korgen, January 3, 2005.

15. Ibid.

16. Dr. Lou Coda, testimonial letter (Los Angeles: Mission Doctors, n.d.).

17. Most Rev. John F. Kinney, *As I Have Done for You* (St. Cloud, MN: Diocese of St. Cloud, 1998), 28.

18. Fr. Bill Vos, interview with Jeffry Odell Korgen, March 3, 2005.

19. Ibid.

20. Shirley Anderson, *Our Mission Connection* (February 2000), 2.

21. Vos, interview.

5. Young Prophets of Justice

1. Some high schools and colleges prefer the term *community-based learning*. In deference to the tradition of *diakonia* in the church, I recommend continuing to use the term *service-learning programs*.

2. Mark Falbo, director of the Center for Community Service at John Carroll University in Cleveland, Ohio, later reminded me that nicotine helps suppress hunger pangs. A hungry person can "bum a cigarette easier than a hamburger," he explained. If I had been prepared and introduced that fact, it might have turned around that conversation among the youth.

3. Robert McCarty, interview with Jeffry Odell Korgen, December 10, 2004.

4. Pamela Reidy, *To Build a Civilization of Love* (Washington, DC: National Catholic Educational Association, 2001), 3.

5. American Academy of Child and Adolescent Psychiatry, "Normal Adolescent Development: Middle School and Early High School Years," *Facts for Families*, no. 57. Available on the aacap.org website.

6. Reidy, *To Build a Civilization of Love*, 7.

7. Ibid., 8.

8. One of the peculiarities of our culture is the extension of adolescence. Among many young adults it appears that late adolescence lingers well into the mid-twenties.

9. American Academy of Child and Adolescent Psychiatry, "Normal Adolescent Development: Late High School Years and Beyond," *Facts for Families*, no. 58. Available on the aacap.org website.

10. Reidy, *To Build a Civilization of Love*, 8.

11. For a helpful review of the World Youth Day statements of Pope John Paul II, including numerous excerpts of the statements, see ibid., chap. 3.

12. John Paul II, "XII World Youth Day, 1997," no. 4. Available at the vatican.va website.

13. McCarty, interview.

14. See "Habitat for Humanity Fact Sheet" on the habitat.org website.

15. Fr. Bill Lies, CSC, interview with Jeffry Odell Korgen, December 30, 2004.

16. Alexander W. Astin, Lori J. Vogelgesang, Elaine K. Ikeda, and Jennifer A. Yee, *How Service Learning Affects Students*, Higher Education Research Institute (Berkeley and Los Angeles: Univ. of California, 2000), executive summary.

17. Ibid.

18. Stephen J. Meyer, Shelley Billig, and Linda Hofschire, "The Impact of K-12 School-Based Service—Learning on Academic Achievement and Student Engagement in Michigan," in *New Perspectives in Service Learning: Research to Advance the Field*, ed. Marshall Welch and Shelley Billig (Greenwich, CT: Information Age Publishing, 2004), 61.

19. Judith Warchal and Ana Ruiz, "The Long-Term Effects of Undergraduate Service-Learning Programs on Postgraduate Employment Choices, Community Engagement, and Civic Leadership," in Welch and Billig, New Perspectives in Service Learning, 88.

20. See Thomas A. Trozzolo, Mary Beckman, and Rebecca Pettit, "The Urban Plunge: College Student Views on Poverty in the U.S.," Research Report 6 (Notre Dame, IN: Center for Social Concerns, January 2004), 1.

21. Lies, interview.

22. Pat Sprankle, interview with Jeffry Odell Korgen, December 29, 2004.

23. Kathleen Maas Weigert, interview with Jeffry Odell Korgen, January 6, 2005.

24. Megan Shepherd, interview with Jeffry Odell Korgen, January 22, 2005.

25. Sr. Linda Campbell, interview with Jeffry Odell Korgen, January 18, 2005.

26. See Joe Holland and Peter Henriot, SJ, *Social Analysis: Linking Faith and Justice* (Maryknoll, NY: Orbis Books, 1988).

27. Sean Lansing, interview with Jeffry Odell Korgen, January 19, 2005.

28. *Faithful Citizenship* is the election-year statement of the Administrative Board of the US Conference of Catholic Bishops.

29. Pam Rector, interview with Jeffry Odell Korgen, January 19, 2005.

30. Sprankle, interview.

31. Shepherd, interview.

6. Broad-Based Community Organizing

1. Tex Sample, *Blue Collar Ministry* (Valley Forge, PA: Judson Press, 1984), 12.

2. Michael Gecan, *Going Public: An Organizer's Guide to Citizen Action* (New York: Random House, 2004), 6.

3. Ibid., 5.

4. Ibid., 56–58.

5. Ibid., 66.

6. Thomas Chabolla, interview with Jeffry Odell Korgen, April 15, 2005.

7. Gecan, *Going Public*, 163.

8. Rosaria Rosado, interview with Jeffry Odell Korgen, March 15, 2005.

9. Ibid.

10. Ibid.

11. Mary Beth Rogers, *Cold Anger: A Story of Faith and Power Politics* (Denton: Univ. of North Texas Press, 1990), 10.

12. Bernard Smith, interview with Jeffry Odell Korgen, March 15, 2005.

13. Institute for Civil Infrastructure Systems, "Asthma and Air Pollution" (Robert F. Wagner Graduate School of Public Service, New York University), available at the icisnyu.org website.

14. Smith, interview.

15. Rosado, interview.

16. Felix Santiago, interview with Jeffry Odell Korgen, March 15, 2005.

17. See Rev. Heidi B. Newmark, *Breathing Space: A Spiritual Journey in the South Bronx* (Boston: Beacon Press, 2003).

18. Santiago, inteview.

19. Ibid.

20. Ibid.

21. Ana Jaquez, interview with Jeffry Odell Korgen, March 29, 2005.

22. José Jimenez, interview with Jeffry Odell Korgen, April 11, 2005.

23. Most Rev. Gerald Walsh, interview with Jeffry Odell Korgen, April 6, 2005.

24. Jaquez, interview.

25. Walsh, interview.

26. Ibid.

27. Virginia Gonzalez, interview with Jeffry Odell Korgen, March 15, 2005.

7. Worker Justice

1. See Jeffry Odell Korgen, "Today's Labor Priests: Four Witnesses for Worker Solidarity," *Church* (Fall 2004), 16–20.

2. Ibid.

3. Ibid.

4. Fr. Michael Gutierrez, homily preached on April 3, 2005, Church of St. Anne, Santa Monica, California.

5. Fr. Michael Gutierrez, interview with Jeffry Odell Korgen, April 3, 2005.

6. Fr. Michael Gutierrez, interview with Jeffry Odell Korgen, April 2, 2005.

7. Gutierrez, interview, April 3, 2005.

8. Ibid.

9. Irene Santiago, interview with Jeffry Odell Korgen, April 2, 2005.

10. Gutierrez, interview, April 2, 2005.

11. Irene Santiago and Fr. Michael Gutierrez, interview with Jeffry Odell Korgen, April 2, 2005.

12. Cynthia Garcia, interview with Jeff Korgen, April 3, 2005.

13. Gutierrez, interview, April 2, 2005.

14. Ibid.

15. Ana G. Jara, interview with Jeffry Odell Korgen, April 2, 2005.

16. Ana Maria Jara, interview with Jeffry Odell Korgen, April 2, 2005.

17. Ana G. Jara, interview,

18. Gutierrez, interview, April 2, 2005.

19. Annie Gomba, interview with Jeffry Odell Korgen, April 3, 2005.

20. Gutierrez, interview, April 2, 2005.

21. Viviana and Yvonne Villegas, interview with Jeffry Odell Korgen, April 3, 2005.

22. For example, after a recent fight between Anglo teens and Hispanic teens, the Anglos were sent home and the Hispanics were arrested.

23. Deacon Raul Molina, interview with Jeffry Odell Korgen, April 3, 2005.

24. As the average age of priestly ordination rises, it is possible that this distinction between priest and laity will diminish. Priests ordained in their mid-thirties tend to have well over a decade of experience in the work force.

25. For more information about Interfaith Worker Justice and its affiliates, see the iwj.org website.